THE WALKING DEAD

THE WALKING DEAD COMICS COMPANION

TITAN

WWW.TITAN-COMICS.COM

**THE WALKING DEAD
COMICS
COMPANION
ISBN: 9781785860102**

Published by Titan,
a division of Titan Publishing Group, Ltd.
144 Southwark Street,
London SE1 0UP.

Collecting material previously
published in The Walking Dead Magazine.

A CIP record for this title is available from the
British Library.

First edition, November 2016

10 9 8 7 6 5 4 3 2 1

Printed in China.

EDITOR Neil Edwards, Toby Weidmann
SENIOR EDITOR Divinia Fleary
DESIGN Russell Seal, Mark Mitchell
ART DIRECTOR Oz Browne
PUBLISHING MANAGER Darryl Tothill
PUBLISHING DIRECTOR Chris Teather
EXECUTIVE DIRECTOR Vivian Cheung
PUBLISHER: Nick Landau

Acknowledgements...
Titan would like the thank everyone at Skybound for
their help in putting this volume together.

CONTENTS

LARGE

WRITING THE CHARACTERS OF *THE WALKING DEAD*

A great story is nothing without great characters to inhabit it. Thankfully, *The Walking Dead* delivers on both fronts, with readers invested in the overall story arc and its lead players. That's all courtesy of one man: Robert Kirkman. As the sole writer on the comic book, everything that happens in the story and all those wonderful (and terrifying) characters we meet are born out of his imagination, before being embellished by the tremendous art of Charlie Adlard. With the comic series passing its 150- issue mark, *TWDM* took the opportunity to pick Kirkman's brain about how he creates, develops and, often, kills off those characters…

WORDS & INTERVIEW:
Tara Bennett

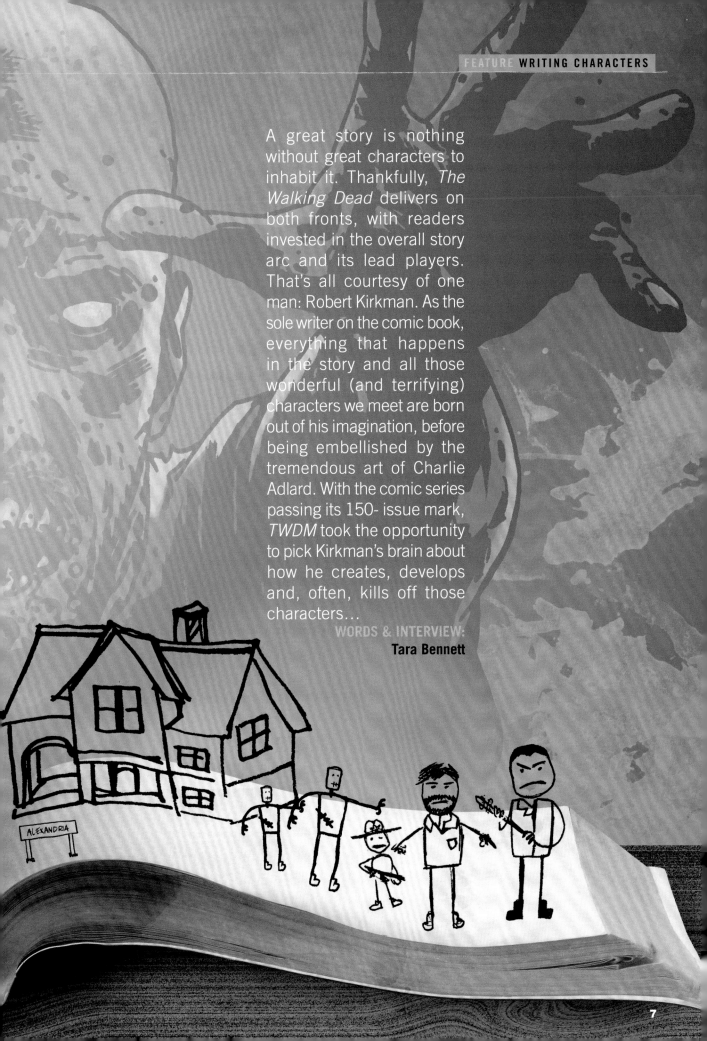

ALEXANDRIA

I n the last few years, Robert Kirkman has added a lot of new titles to his résumé: executive producer, development executive and co-partner of Skybound. He's also the go-to guy when it comes to media interviews about his various TV series, AMC's *The Walking Dead*, AMC's *Fear The Walking Dead* and the upcoming *Outcast*. But when you ask Kirkman which of his titles define him the best, he readily answers "writer."

A comic book creator going back to 2000, Kirkman has been cranking out fresh stories every year, if not every month, for a decade and a half. With *Invincible* and *The Walking Dead* alone, Kirkman has more than 270 issues to his name, and that doesn't include his other series, one-shots and previous Marvel Comics work.

Since finding the story is what sustains him daily, *TWDM* sat down to talk with Kirkman about his personal writing process...

Let's start with characters; what's your process for creating them, from conception through to briefing Charlie Adlard about their look?
It's different for different characters. It really runs the gamut. Negan, for instance, I knew I was introducing him with the name Negan, I knew what he was going to do to Glenn, but [at that point] I don't think I had decided it would be with a baseball bat or not.

Charlie had done the covers for [issues] 97 to 102 all in one chunk early, so we had them for marketing. All of those covers had Saviors holding their weapons, with their heads cut off at the top so you couldn't see their faces. You saw these

"IT HAPPENS ORGANICALLY. I WANT TO ADD ANOTHER CHARACTER INTO THE MIX... WE'LL SEE HOW IT COMES OUT, BUT WE MIGHT HAVE JUST COME UP WITH A NEW, COOL CHARACTER."

scary-looking, geared-up dudes with terrifying weapons. I basically sent him a list: "One guy has a crossbow, another has a chainsaw, another has a bloody machete, another has a baseball bat with barbed wire around it, and another guy has this..."

When the cover came in for 100, I don't think it was intended to be the cover because I think he was going to do all six and then I was going to pick which covers were which. I was like, "Oh, that guy with the baseball bat has a cool jacket. I think I'll make that guy Negan." It happened like that.

So you don't have a visual idea for all your characters?
It's weird. For some of the most important characters, I haven't given [Charlie] very much direction at all. I think with the Governor I was like, "It's just a guy," and he drew a guy walking into frame with the handlebar mustache and the long hair. I don't think I described him at all. But with Michonne, I did some sketches and she had dreadlocks. So it just depends.

> "MICHELANGELO WOULD SAY ABOUT CARVING SCULPTURES: 'IT WAS ALWAYS THERE, I JUST HAD TO FIND IT IN THE STONE.' I REALLY LIKE THAT PROCESS WHEN IT COMES TO DEVELOPING CHARACTERS."

I was writing a cover description just this last Sunday, because Charlie is doing a new batch of covers. In the cover description, I wrote, "These people are doing this and this is happening and let's make this character somebody important who shows up." I was just riffing about this and that and was like, "Whoa! This might be a pretty big character."

It happens organically like that. I knew there was a hole in the book and I wanted to add another character into the mix. We'll see how it comes out and what happens with it, but we might have just come up with a new, cool character that people will be talking about.

Do you write a bible, or a deep character background, for your characters and world, to keep track of everything?

As far as writing bibles, aside from that being a lot of work, first and foremost I'm trying to have fun. I can make this sound 'artsy-fartsy' by referring to Michelangelo carving sculptures. He would say, "It was always there, I just had to find it in the stone," which

> "IF A CHARACTER HAS A DISTINCTIVE VOICE AND SPEAKS IN A CERTAIN WAY, I LET THAT EVOLVE OVER TIME"

is what he would tell people who would give him compliments. I really like that process when it comes to developing characters.

My entry for a character such as Jesus is that he's 'a cool Kung Fu guy, that he's got long hair and a beard.' As I am writing those issues, I like to dig deeper into that stone and find what's there as I am telling the story. I like to keep things as vague and loose as possible, not because I'm lazy – although I *am* lazy – but because I like being able, as I'm writing the character, to go this way and that way.

There's a lot of Michonne's back-story that is being used now, with her daughters and ex-husband. I didn't have that stuff planned out when she walked though that field with those zombies. But all of that stuff is very valuable to her story and useful to her story now. If I had written a bible and nailed a bunch of stuff down, I might be writing now thinking, 'Ugh! It doesn't fit.' I like to keep things organic.

Do you find it easy to create the voice of a character on the page?

There is so much to a voice that doesn't really exist in comics. The way a person speaks, the speed at which they speak and the way they string their words together, which we do in television, doesn't really apply to comics.

For instance, Andrew Lincoln has a unique, distinctive, sometimes odd way he talks as Rick Grimes, which is something

UNDERSTOOD, I THINK THAT'S ENOUGH FIGHTING. PLEASE ALLOW ME TO INTRODUCE MYSELF.

MY NAME IS PAUL MONROE...

...BUT MY FRIENDS HAVE TAKEN TO CALLING ME JESUS.

WRAKK!

he's crafted as a big part of that character. But that doesn't exist in the comics.

I can have characters in the comic with personal ticks, such as Axel saying, "You follow me?" all the time. Different things like that can be done in the dialogue to give somebody a distinct character. I do try to come up with the way people say or don't say things. But as far as coming up with a character and trying to build a unique way of speaking, that is not feasible. I have a thousand characters in the book. What can you do?

But I do try to make sure that when you're reading the dialogue in the comic books, if you were just to look at the balloons, hopefully, most of the time, you should be able to know who is talking. But let's be honest, that's probably not the case. (*Laughs*)

What about when a character is allowed to mature as a person?
One thing I do try to pay attention to is with a character such as Maggie, if you go back to when she was introduced, she immediately had a voice. The things she said were very much in line with who she was. But if you were to compare Maggie from issue 20 to issue 135, she's speaking differently. She's grown as a person and has more authority.

Even if a character has a distinctive voice and does speak a certain way, I let that evolve over time. These characters are going through a lot and they are growing and changing and learning. I do try to illustrate that as much as possible in the way they speak.

> **"TRYING TO BUILD A UNIQUE WAY OF SPEAKING [FOR EVERY CHARACTER] IS NOT FEASIBLE. I HAVE A THOUSAND CHARACTERS IN THE BOOK. WHAT CAN YOU DO?"**

You are a fixture at cons and meet a lot of people. Do you take inspiration for characters from real people you encounter?

Yeah, that happens all the time. I do that more now that I'm doing a lot of meetings in LA because you meet a lot of people. There are certainly turns of phrases, or things people do, or mannerisms they have that I'm like, "I gotta get a character who does this or does that."

There are definitely a few – I won't point out who they are – but there are definitely a few people over the course of *The Walking Dead* who I've thought had really interesting or unique characteristics which I've incorporated into someone [the comic characters]. It's kind of fun to make a fake construct of a person you like, or don't like, and then dictate how they live their lives and how they die, if that doesn't sound too psychotic.

A lot of your characters have very specific professions – cops, engineers, doctors – or they encounter very real situations. Do you research a lot for detail?

What interests me the most is the characters, so I do as much research as I have to do to make sure the characters and stories are interesting. The book is real to me. Also, it's important to me that, aside from the zombies, everything is real. I do as much reading as I can, like finding out about agriculture and things like that. It's not fun but it's somewhat necessary.

As far as the doctor stuff goes, I think the best example was in issue 64. I wanted to show Eugene was really smart and I wanted to have him do some kind of MacGyver thing. I started researching the easiest way to field dress a wound.

"THERE ARE CERTAINLY TURNS OF PHRASES, OR THINGS PEOPLE DO, OR MANNERISMS THEY HAVE THAT I'M LIKE, 'I GOTTA GET A CHARACTER WHO DOES THAT.'"

What I wanted was something complicated and impressive so people would think, 'Eugene is really smart – look at that!' But then I found out the thing you need to do to clean a bullet wound is wash it out with water. By doing the research, the accurate thing for Eugene to say was, "OK, lay him down. Someone get me a bucket of water to wash this thing out." It seems lazy and fake but if you had no other resources, keeping the wound clean is all that matters.

That was lame, so I decided to write it inaccurately. I had him ask for tea leaves and candle wax, and he crumpled the leaves on the wound to draw out whatever moisture was there. People wrote into the comic saying, "That is going to cause gangrene and a surefire way to lead to amputation!" I just didn't put those letters in the letters column. But the 90 percent of people who aren't doctors thought Eugene was a smart guy!

If *The Walking Dead* leads to a few leg amputations, as long as the story was interesting, that's a risk I'm willing to take. (*Laughs*)

Does your ease of writing a character ever determine how long they last in the story?

It certainly doesn't keep me from killing them, because I've killed a lot of characters I didn't want to kill as I felt it was the right time to do it. Sometimes I regret that, but whatever... I end up introducing another character maybe I love more, or not.

There are certainly characters that are more fun to write. Negan is really fun to write. When Rick is doing really crazy things, he's fun to write. Carl is fun to write. Andrea. I think the

characters that get the most 'screen time' in the comic book are the ones I enjoy writing the most. I prefer writing scenes more than the individuals in the scene. Sometimes I'm really invested in a scene and it doesn't matter who the characters are as long as it's coming together.

Your villains are very distinctive in *The Walking Dead*, but do you sometimes have to double-check that a new villain isn't repeating what a previous one did?
I think it's easy for me because there's a purpose to each villain and they are trying to accomplish a different thing.

> "I'VE KILLED A LOT OF CHARACTERS I DIDN'T WANT TO KILL AS I FELT IT WAS THE RIGHT TIME TO DO IT. SOMETIMES I REGRET THAT."

That is clear to me and always present on my mind. But it's not necessarily something the audience is aware of. Because the characters are serving a different function, there really isn't any overlap. I think it's easy to keep them pretty straight.

As I say that, I am worried that there's an issue where Alpha does something exactly like the Governor. I try not to let that happen.

Are there any attributes you feel a writer needs to possess?
A work ethic, I guess. I'm not an expert on writing or an expert on writers so it's hard for me to say. I've heard the quote, "I don't enjoy writing. I enjoy having written." I would say I disagree with that. I enjoy writing quite a bit.

I would say try to enjoy what you are doing and maybe it will come through in the work. And have a work ethic. Most people are lazy, so if you have a work ethic at all, you have a leg-up on most. •

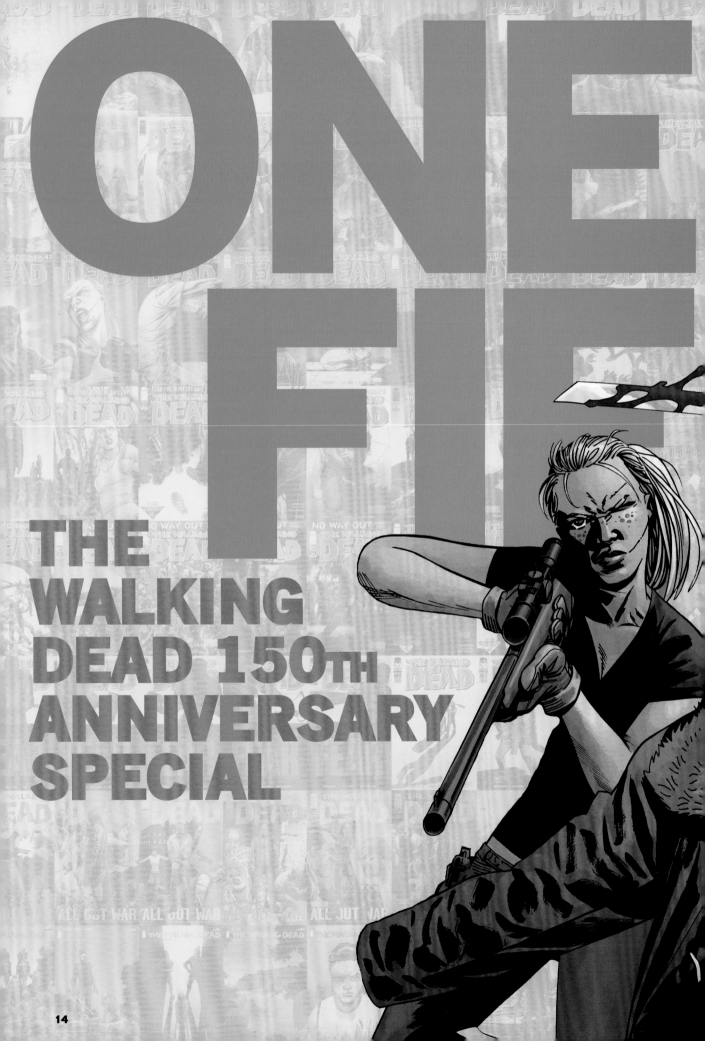

ONE FIF

THE WALKING DEAD 150TH ANNIVERSARY SPECIAL

HUNDRED AND TY!

WHEN ROBERT KIRKMAN SAT DOWN ONE DAY TO PEN THE FIRST ISSUE OF A SMALL INDIE ZOMBIE COMIC, HE COULD SCARCELY HAVE DREAMT THAT NOT ONLY WOULD IT STILL BE GOING 149 ISSUES LATER, BUT THAT IT WOULD ALSO BECOME A WORLDWIDE PHENOMENON. WITH THE COMIC HAVING PASSED THE 150-ISSUE MILESTONE, *TWDM* DECIDED WE SHOULD TAKE A LOOK AT SOME OF OUR HIGHLIGHTS FROM THE SERIES OVER THE YEARS. WE'VE PICKED 15 OF OUR FAVORITE MOMENTS, LIMITING OURSELVES TO A CHOICE OF JUST ONE FROM EVERY 10 ISSUES... **WORDS:** NICK JONES

15

"I'M PREGNANT."

ISSUES: 1-10
MOMENT: ISSUE #7

It may seem perverse to single out for special praise one of the quietest of the initial 10 issues of *The Walking Dead*, especially when the preceding six issues boast roamers galore, the debuts of a bunch of key characters – not least Rick Grimes himself – and Carl Grimes shooting Shane dead. But #7 is a pivotal issue, seeing the group of survivors setting out on the road, the introduction of Tyreese, and Lori telling Rick she's pregnant, almost certainly with the offspring of Shane, whose grave she spat on at the start of the issue – and all this on Christmas Day. Above all that, this issue marks the debut of artist Charlie Adlard, the beginning of an unbroken writer/artist run which stands as one of the most remarkable achievements in modern comics.

"STAY CLOSE TO ME."

ISSUES: 11-20
MOMENT: ISSUE #19

The series is nothing if not eventful in its teens, as Rick and his group uncover the secret of Hershel's barn, establish a new home in the prison, deal with a horrifying suicide pact – and an even more horrifying double (or, more accurately, twin) murder – and almost carry out a lynching. All this pales in comparison, however, to the introduction of one of the most popular characters the series has ever seen: Michonne – garbed in a makeshift cape, with tethered and partially dismembered walkers in tow, hacking and slashing her way into Rick and co's lives and readers' hearts.

"WE ARE THE WALKING DEAD!"

ISSUES: 21-30
MOMENT: ISSUE #24

Zombie horror comic though it may be, *The Walking Dead* is as memorable for what the characters say and do as for the roamer-related shocks. The comic's #20s bring attempted suicide, rape, an epic brawl between Rick and Tyreese, the introduction of Woodbury and the Governor, and not one but two distressing dismemberments – Allen's in #21 and Rick himself's in #28 – but issue #24 features an electrifying speech from Rick in which he lays bare the reality of the situation: there is no rescue coming, the world has forever changed and the survivors are all living on borrowed time. In other words, *they* are the walking dead.

"DON'T LOOK BACK, CARL!"
ISSUES: 41–50
MOMENT: ISSUE #48

The battle with the Governor's forces has raged for four issues, costing Tyreese his life and bringing the prison community to the brink of disaster. All of that is merely a prelude to the wholesale slaughter of issue #48, however, as the prison perimeter is breached and one by one Patricia, Billy, Alice, and then Hershel are killed. But the most shocking deaths of all are those of Lori Grimes and baby Judith, mercilessly gunned down as they race along in Rick and Carl's wake. The one consolation? The Governor buys it too, shot in the head by Lori and Judith's killer, Lilly Caul.

"I THINK WE'LL START WITH THIS."
ISSUES: 31–40 MOMENT: ISSUE #33

The 33rd issue must surely rank as one of the most traumatic – and yet cathartic – of the entire series. Midway through Rick, Glenn and co's escape from Woodbury, Michonne breaks away from the group in order to go back and confront the man who raped and tortured her: the Governor. Upon finding him, she fights him, strips him, ties him up and then shows him a succession of implements – including pliers, a spoon and an electric power drill – which she intends to use on him. She then proceeds to do just that... For most of the remainder of the issue.

"RICK… YOU MADE IT."
ISSUES: 61–70
MOMENT: ISSUE #69

After all the trauma of the #60s – cannibalism, gruesome executions, Dale's death, child-on-child infanticide – the final pages of issue 69 offer a welcome ray of hope, as Rick's group arrive at the walled community of Alexandria. That said, by contrast the last leg of the journey depicted in this issue is utterly terrifying, involving an unscheduled stop in Washington, DC, to rescue a pair of stranded Alexandria foragers; although it does afford us an opportunity to see what's become of the capital. Unsurprisingly, it's nothing good: the dilapidated city is overrun with walkers.

"OH MY GOD…"
ISSUES: 51–60
MOMENT: ISSUE #59

There have been many instances of roamers grouping together prior to this point, but this issue marks the first appearance of a full-blown herd, a phenomenon that will plague our protagonists henceforth. As Rick, Carl, Abraham, and Morgan drive back to the main group of survivors, they crest a rise and are met by the terrifying sight of hundreds upon hundreds of the undead ranging across the landscape and blocking the road. Forced to abandon their vehicle after first attempting to drive through the dense pack of walkers, the group fight their way through the horde and run for their lives.

"WHAT THE HELL IS GOING ON HERE?"
ISSUES: 71–80
MOMENT: ISSUE #75

Since the early days, Robert Kirkman had been promising in the Letter Hacks column that if the series ever made it to issue 75, aliens would turn up in the story. True to his word, they do... kinda. In a brilliant (non-canon) post-letters coda – drawn by Ryan Ottley, artist on Kirkman's superhero series *Invincible* – Rick vanishes after being thumped by Michonne, wakes up in a UFO with a robot hand, dons a heroic costume and discovers that the undead are all part of a diabolical invasion plot spearheaded by a cyborg Governor. *Now* it all makes sense...

"DAD?"
ISSUES: 81–90 MOMENT: ISSUE #83

Horror is heaped upon horror in issue #83. Alexandria's walls have been breached and the community overrun by the undead, leaving a small group – including Rick, Carl, Rick's new lover Jessie and her young son, Ron – trapped in Rick's house. Rick takes the rash decision that they must leave and leads the group through the walker multitudes, smeared in zombie gunk to fool the walkers. It doesn't work: a terrified Ron is grabbed and bitten, then Jessie. But as she's overwhelmed by the undead, Jessie won't let go of Carl's arm – so Rick hacks her hand off to save his son. And then, to cap it all, a stray bullet blows off part of Carl's head. Blimey!

"MAGGIE!"
ISSUES: 91–100
MOMENT: ISSUE #100

A milestone, and the biggest-selling issue of *The Walking Dead* to date – not to mention the bestselling comic of 2012 – with an array of all-star artist variant covers, issue 100 also boasts the introduction of foul-mouthed sociopath, and leader of the Saviors, Negan, and one of the most gut-churning demises of the entire series. The tension as Negan decides which of Rick's band will die is unbearable, and the seven-page sequence where he chooses Glenn, one of the series' most beloved characters, and then beats him to death with Lucille, Negan's barbed wire-wrapped baseball bat, while Glenn's wife, Maggie, looks on helplessly, is both sickening and haunting.

"OH, I THINK I FORGOT TO MENTION... EZEKIEL HAS A TIGER."
ISSUES: 101–110
MOMENT: ISSUE #108

In a world where the dead getting up and walking is an everyday occurrence, it's perhaps understandable that a sense of the absurdity of life is generally in short supply. Not in this issue, however, which introduces not only the larger-than-life Ezekiel, self-styled King of, well, the Kingdom, but also Ezekiel's tame(ish) tiger, Shiva. It's fairly safe to assume that with everything Rick's been through, he must have figured nothing else could surprise him by now, so the look on his face when he first sets eyes on the pair of them is priceless.

"…I BELIEVE IN RICK GRIMES."
ISSUES: 111-120
MOMENT: ISSUE #118

Falling in the middle of the epic 'All Out War' storyline – a desperate struggle for survival pitting the combined forces of Alexandria, the Hilltop and the Kingdom against Negan and the Saviors – this issue details two assaults on Savior outposts: a successful one by a group led by Rick, and a disastrous one by a group led by Ezekiel, which leaves everyone dead bar Ezekiel himself, who only survives due to Shiva's sacrifice. But it's most memorable for the line that Maggie utters when faced with Hilltop leader Gregory's cowardice: "If there's *one* thing in this world that I'm certain of… I know *this*… *I believe in Rick Grimes.*"

"DO YOU STILL WANT TO KILL ME?"
ISSUES: 121–130
MOMENT: ISSUE #127

Sure, the showdown with Negan outside Alexandria's gates in issues 125 and 126 is outstanding, and there are good arguments for either one of those issues being the best of the #120s. For sheer bravado, though, issue 127 is hard to beat. Punting the narrative on by two years is an audacious move on the part of Kirkman and Adlard, and yet it works, in part because it throws up so many burning questions (not least being where the hell Michonne is). Best of all is the closing three-page conversation between Negan and Carl, a tantalising mix of animosity and, curiously, kinship.

"WE WHISPER AND THE DEAD DON'T MIND."
ISSUES: 131-140
MOMENT: ISSUE #132

Following on from the jolting revelation of zombies that can apparently talk in issue 130, here comes the further revelation that they wield knives too, as Dante's search party – sent out by Maggie to find Ken – is surrounded by walkers who suddenly start stabbing them. The slight disappointment engendered by Dante's realization that these aren't actually walkers is quickly tempered by the explanation of what they really are: people, clad in the putrefying, stitched-together skins of the undead. These are the Whisperers, and they're not like us…

"RICK… WHAT DO WE DO NOW?"
ISSUES: 141-150 MOMENT: ISSUE #144

Having been threatened by Alpha, the leader of the Whisperers, with the biggest herd of walkers ever seen and ordered not to cross into the Whisperers' territory again, Rick is allowed to leave with Carl – Rick's reason for intruding onto their turf – and Alpha's daughter, Lydia. It's only when they reach the border of the Whisperers' region that Rick comprehends Alpha's comment about marking that border: impaled on spikes are the severed heads of 12 Alexandria, Hilltop and Kingdom denizens and Saviors members, including Ezekiel and Rosita (who was pregnant). Clearly, this does not bode well for relations between Rick's people and Alpha's…

DRAWN OF THE DEAD

While the zombie is by no means a new addition to fiction – some suggest the concept dates back 2,000 years – it has certainly come into its own over the past 50 years and is now, through films, TV shows, books and, of course, comics, firmly ingrained in popular culture.

GUH.

When *The Walking Dead* comic launched in 2003, it surprised many people who had been brought up suckling on the bloated teat of garish superhero stories, by choosing to depict its apocalyptic world, and its cadaverous denizens, in black and white. Such is its unique identity, it's now hard to imagine *The Walking Dead* comic any other way, and the man largely responsible for that is artist Charlie Adlard. But after so many years of illustrating the damned things, surely he's starting to run out of ideas on how to keep the undead looking so, er, alive? Not one bit, he tells *TWDM*. WORDS & INTERVIEW: Dan Auty

Horror comics are part of a tradition that stretches as far back as those featuring superheroes. From the pulp magazines of the 1920s through adaptations of classic monsters and the huge popularity of EC's taboo-busting output in the 1940s and 1950s, the comic book has proved itself to be a perfect medium for telling scary stories.

But unlike their superhero-drawing contemporaries, pioneering horror artists are long forgotten, perhaps because the controversy over their work in the first half of the 20th Century meant that the horror comic spent several decades in relative obscurity. It is only with a more recent resurgence of horror-themed comic books that artists specializing in the darker side of things have started to become recognized for their work – and none more so than *The Walking Dead* illustrator Charlie Adlard.

Adlard is in the unusual position of having been the sole artist for more than 90 per cent of the book's nine-year run, picking up artistic duties on the title from issue seven, way back in 2004. It's rare to find a book of such popularity and longevity that has maintained the same artist for so long, but this is a major part of the series' strength. There's little doubt that consistency in both the

"The challenge is to make the page look interesting. That's where I really thrive."

writing and the artwork has helped the book build and maintain its devoted fan base.

Adlard himself knew *The Walking Dead* writer Robert Kirkman having drawn Joe Casey's superhero noir *Codeflesh* for Kirkman's company, Funkotron, but although he does describe himself as a horror fan, it wasn't the zombie content that drew him in.

"Robert got me between jobs," says the UK-based artist. "The burning desire wasn't there for me to do a zombie book, personally. But then I read the script and realized it was more than just a zombie story."

It may have been *The Walking Dead*'s powerful drama that led Adlard to the project, but his skills as a depicter of violent, gore-splattered zombie action have, nevertheless, created some unforgettable horror imagery.

Although Kirkman carefully plots each issue, Adlard is given plenty of freedom to depict the story's undead mayhem in a way that he thinks will work best on the page.

"Robert is not a particularly detailed writer, which is how I like it," he says. "I think we both respect each other's skill sets. Very rarely will I criticize or critique his writing, and vice versa. There tends to be a bit more description in the action scenes – because, obviously, Robert has an idea of what's going to happen and I haven't – so I need to know roughly where things are going. But in terms of 'camera angles', it's left up to me to do pretty much what I want. I will sometimes get an instruction, such as 'pull back' or 'show this from the middle distance', but apart from that it's pretty much what I decide to do."

OH,
JESUS--
I--IT
CAN'T--

The living dead might exist as background to the dramatic interaction between Kirkman's characters, but there's no denying that over the space of nine years Adlard has drawn a lot of them. From epic double-page spreads of zombie hordes to close-up detail on individual walkers, the artist has ensured that fans don't just get the same identikit zombie every time. Nevertheless – and especially considering the speed at which each issue must be turned around – the process of actually drawing zombies comes relatively easily to the artist.

Adlard states: "I don't consciously go out every time thinking I must draw each zombie differently. I, more or less, make them up as I go along – I literally let my hand go for it, and my brain follows second. Simply, in terms of the act of drawing, you're going to come up with different faces each time. That said, if there's a zombie that's more than just background – an important zombie that leads a plot point somewhere – I do tend to consider the look of that one a bit more and think 'I haven't done *that* type of person yet'."

"Zombies are the most gory of all the 'classic' monsters. *The Walking Dead* world is not a nice, sweet place."

HUMNGH.

However, Adlard reveals that one aspect he does consider when drawing the living dead is the specific level of decay that the walkers have undergone as the comic's timeline progresses.

He explains: "Our zombies are slowly decaying, so what I'm half self-consciously trying to do is, the further we get down the line with the story, the more decayed and monstrous they will look. There are more of them that have been around for two or three years, as opposed to fresh, new zombies, because most of the people died in the initial plague. So, I'm conscious of slightly upping the decay more as we progress through the story."

PAUSE FOR TALK

But what of those issues where zombie action does take a backseat? Much of *The Walking Dead*'s conflict and drama comes not from its heroes running away from the undead, but from trying to exist within a tense, fragile alliance that is constantly on the verge of breaking down. Is there a challenge in keeping dialogue, drama-heavy issues as visually interesting as those packed with action?

"In a lot of ways, that's what I enjoy more than the action sequences," explains Adlard. "Action scenes, although time-consuming, are often quite easy to draw. They almost draw themselves – I can usually see them instantly on the page, and then it's just a matter of physically drawing them. Quieter scenes, however, require a lot more thought and invention to make them interesting.

"It's very easy to do quiet talking scenes in a movie or on television. You have an establishing shot, followed by a close-up of person A talking to person B, and you switch back and forth between them. It's the dialogue and the actors that make the piece interesting.

"But with a comic," Adlard continues, "it would be incredibly dull to do that all the time. So, the challenge for me is it to make the page look interesting, or at least do something with the talking heads – a change of mood or something. That's where I really thrive and get my inspirational chops from."

THRIFTY SHADES OF GRAY

As well as legendary movie poster illustrators such as Bob Peak and Robert McGinnis, many of Adlard's influences come from comic book artists who have worked in black and white. His striking use of monochrome has continued to develop from his early work in the 1990s on much-loved British sci-fi weekly *2000AD*, and his use of the form to create mood and tension is widely regarded to be among the finest in the industry.

"It can be disturbing when I read the script, but by the time I come to draw it I'm not having nightmares. It's just marks on paper."

Adlard is truly old school when it comes to his artistic tools, relying almost entirely on pens and brushes instead of more modern digital means. "I think if I had to work electronically it would actually slow me down," he admits. "I do occasional bits of electronic work – jigging things about a bit or for repeat panels, when it would be an utter waste of time to redraw exactly the same thing. Those times I might as well do the same panel in Photoshop. But 99.9 per cent of it is still physical."

One additional bonus of illustrating a horror book in black and white is the ability to showcase some truly disturbing imagery in a way that might not be possible were *The Walking Dead* in color. The scenes of zombie carnage – not to mention violence between human characters – certainly push the boundaries at times, and Adlard understands that black and white is perhaps a more effective way to show this.

He explains: "*The Walking Dead* is a realistic book – apart from the zombies! – so, if it was in color, I think I'd want to color it as realistically as possible. It would, therefore, have more impact, because instead of that brighter red 'comic book' blood, it would be a proper, darker shade. Then, I think perhaps we might not be able to get away with as much. By taking away the color, we're giving ourselves a bit more leeway."

To Adlard's knowledge, neither he nor Kirkman have ever been asked to tone down the book's graphic content, but he is a firm advocate of the power of suggestion over showing every last gory detail. "If I can, I'll stick it off-screen," he says. "Not because I'm a prude or anything, but because I believe people conjure up worse images in their heads than you could possibly draw. The monster is universally disappointing once you see it in full. I always think it's best to keep it in the shadows."

Nevertheless, the artist is well aware that the very subject matter of *The Walking Dead* does require him to draw some pretty brutal stuff.

"We are making a zombie book, and by their very nature, zombies are the most gory of all the 'classic' monsters. And there is reason to show some of the violence explicitly – these are characters you've lived with for so long that it has much more impact if you really show what happens to them. This world is not a nice, sweet place."

GOODBYE KITTY

Having brought Kirkman's often disturbing visions to life for so long, Adlard says that he doesn't really have a problem with this side of his role in *The Walking Dead* process. The impact of the storyline is dealt with, and mentally processed, when he receives the scripts for each issue, so by the time he's actually sat at a drawing board, there isn't that emotional element attached to it. As he says: "It's just marks on paper."

He adds: "I could literally be drawing someone going out and culling 25 white kittens in the most brutal manner you can imagine – it wouldn't matter what I'm drawing – it is just pen and ink. It can be disturbing when I read the script, but by the time I come to draw it, I'm not getting nightmares."

The only time Adlard had any discussion with Kirkman about what he was being asked to draw came with issue 33, in which Michonne extracts her horrific revenge on The Governor. This was an extreme sequence even by the standards of *The Walking Dead*, and one that caused considerable controversy among fans – though ironically the issue also stands as one of the biggest-selling of the entire series.

"That was more of a bone of contention with me than anything else," he says. "I did question if we needed to unrelentingly draw this thing for 10 to 15 pages or so. But Robert explained it and I appreciated his reasoning. But sometimes I think we could have shown not as much."

THE BEST OF THE BEST

Nearly a decade down the line, Adlard and Kirkman's working relationship is clearly a highly efficient one, allowing them to maintain the fast pace needed to produce a high quality comic every month. He says the fact that they live on different continents makes no difference to the process: "I could live in the Arctic so long as I have an Internet connection, a scanner, a computer and a drawing board. Or I could live next door to him, and we'd probably collaborate in the same way."

While Adlard is largely left to his own devices, occasionally Kirkman does get more particular with what he wants. When asked about a personal favorite among all the zombie drawings, Adlard laughs while recalling a specific request from the writer. "It's in Issue 78," the artist recalls, "when the zombie horde assembles before attacking Alexandria. There's a big double-page shot of them all gathering in the street in Washington DC, and I remember Robert writing a fairly short description in the script – 'The zombies assemble in a street in DC', followed by a few other notes. But then he finished off by saying, 'Make this the best thing you've ever drawn!'

"I thought, 'That's not going to happen!' As soon as you set out to draw the best thing you've ever drawn, it will never be that. The best things you draw are the ones that just... happen. But as it turns out, it probably was one of the best spreads I had worked on up to that point. It's still one I use in promotion." •

CHOICE CUTS

ENEMY MINE

This 'Choice Cuts' is not dedicated to one individual, but to several characters who all have one thing in common: a hatred for our hero, Rick. With Negan making his presence felt in AMC's TV series, it's time to take a look at Rick Grimes' greatest foes.

WORDS: Dan Auty

SHANE WALSH

Shane was never as big a physical threat to Rick as many of the subsequent enemies, and the unlucky deputy didn't even make it beyond issue six. But the swift unraveling of his relationship with Rick and his ensuing death proved pivotal in the way that Rick dealt with this dangerous new world.

Rick barely had time to register that Shane had enjoyed a brief affair with his wife before his son Carl shot him in the neck. But Shane's breakdown and the anger with which he turned on his former best friend and work colleague continues to haunt Rick, having shaken his trust in people and forcing him to abandon many of the principles of law and morality that he had previously upheld.

When Rick realized that it was not a zombie bite that caused reanimation and that anyone who was killed would return, he set about digging up Shane's grave, unable to reconcile that his friend was still moving under the earth.

"I don't know why you did what you did. But you were a good man," he told the Zombie Shane as he emerged from the grave, before putting a final bullet between his eyes. "But I ain't gonna bury you again."

"EVERYTHING WAS SO PERFECT, UNTIL YOU CAME BACK... YOU WEREN'T MEANT TO COME BACK. YOU WEREN'T MEANT TO LIVE!" SHANE

PHILIP BLAKE

Probably the most notable villain in *The Walking Dead* – certainly for the first 50 issues – is The Governor. A case could be made for Michonne being the mustachioed tyrant's true nemesis, but Rick certainly had some life-changing encounters with the man also known as Philip Blake.

From their very first encounter, it was clear that these men were flipsides of the same coin – both charismatic leaders who would do anything necessary to maintain the status quo. But while Rick just wanted to keep his family and friends alive, The Governor strove to maintain his iron grip on the people of Woodbury. He demonstrated the depths to which he would stoop during their first meeting, when The Governor chopped off Rick's right hand. This set about a battle of wills between the two men that eventually drove The Governor to lead an assault on Rick's prison stronghold. The repercussions of this final encounter would last well beyond The Governor's lifetime.

"I WILL GET WHAT I WANT. THERE IS NOTHING YOU CAN DO TO PREVENT ME. DO I MAKE MYSELF CLEAR?" THE GOVERNOR

THIS!

I KNEW NONE OF YOU WOULD *WANT* TO SEE THIS, AND I APOLOGIZE FOR SHOCKING YOU.

I JUST WANT TO MAKE YOU ALL COMPLETELY AWARE OF THE KIND OF PEOPLE WE'RE DEALING WITH...

I'M GLAD TO SEE YOU FEEL THE SAME WAY.

...BUT THERE HAS TO BE *SOMEONE* HERE WHO HAS AT LEAST A PASSING FAMILIARITY WITH THIS GENERAL AREA. IF YOU DO--PLEASE LET ME KNOW.

FIRST WE NEED TO *FIND* THEM. I KNOW MOST OF THE PEOPLE WHO LIVED IN THIS AREA MIGRATED TO ATLANTA WHEN THE GOVERNMENT ORDERED US ALL INTO THE CITIES...

THE PRISON THEY LIVE IN COULD BE FIVE MILES AWAY-- OR IT COULD BE FIFTEEN, AND WE'RE NOT EVEN SURE OF WHICH DIRECTION IT'S IN. THIS IS NOT GOING TO BE EASY.

BUT IT WILL GET DONE--THEY *WILL* BE PUNISHED. OF THAT, YOU CAN BE SURE.

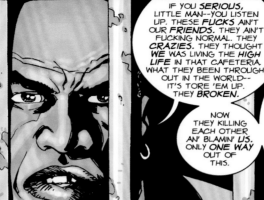

RICK'S GREATEST ENEMIES FACT FILE

NAMES: Shane, Dexter and Thomas, The Governor, The Hunters, Negan and The Saviors

AGES: Various, although strangely all are roughly in their 30s and 40s

JOBS: Police sheriff, criminal, governor, cannibal, mobster

LIKES: Lori and Carl, murder, collecting heads, the taste of human flesh, power

DISLIKES: Rick

FIRST APPEARANCES: Shane – issue one (comics), season one, episode one: 'Days Gone By' (TV series); Dexter and Thomas – issue 13 (comics), officially not in the TV series, but similar characters first appeared in season three, episode one: 'Seed' (TV series); The Governor – issue 27 (comics), season three, episode three: 'Walk With Me' (TV series); The Hunters – issue 63 (comics), n/a (TV series); Negan and The Saviors – issue 98 (comics), n/a (TV series)

CURRENT STATUS: Shane – dead (both); Dexter and Thomas – dead (comics), n/a (TV); The Governor – dead (comics), alive (TV); The Hunters – dead (comics), n/a (TV); Negan and The Saviors – alive (comics), n/a (TV)

DEXTER AND THOMAS

Rick's time in the prison, inevitably, forced our hero to face some individuals every bit as dangerous as the walkers outside for the first time. On the face of it, Dexter was the more unstable of the two inmates, doing time for the murder of his wife and her lover. But, ultimately, it was Thomas who proved to be the true menace – an insane psychopath. His initially calm exterior gave way to a sadistic bloodlust when he decapitated Hershel's twin daughters.

Once a man who believed in justice and due process, Rick's encounters with these two were the final confirmation that the old rules no longer applied in this savage world. Blaming himself for the girls' death – having promised Hershel that they would be safe in the prison – he savagely beat Thomas before deciding that he should be hung by the neck until dead. Dexter got off relatively lightly: Rick quietly shot him during a zombie skirmish, putting a swift end to the inmate's attempted coup.

CHRIS AND THE HUNTERS

The cannibalistic survivors calling themselves the Hunters only featured in *The Walking Dead* for a handful of issues, but like Shane or Thomas, their conflict with Rick led to another seismic shift in the way we perceive him.

Realizing that there was only one way to stop these living flesh-munchers from targeting his group, Rick went to confront their leader, Chris. The latter's refusal to back down forced Rick – with the help of Andrea, Abraham and Michonne (and a watching, horrified Gabriel) – to slaughter the whole gang. The look on Rick's face in the silent aftermath, as they burnt the bodies, said it all – he has long since passed the point of no return. When it comes to protecting his loved ones, there is no room for compromise or remorse.

NEGAN AND THE SAVIORS

The Saviors, led by the mysterious, sadistic Negan, present the latest threat to Rick and those under his command. When Rick first encountered some of this brutal army of survivalists, he dealt with them in his now usual way – he killed all but one, sending the remaining man back to tell the others that the Hilltop community was now under his protection.

But Rick made a fatal error, completely misjudging the size, strength and will of Negan's men. The following retaliation, which results in the horrific murder of one of the original survivors, Glenn, led our flawed hero to question whether resorting to violence was always the best way to protect the group. He found an ally in Michonne, who told him: "I never fought to fight... I fought to live. If you're sitting here telling me the smart move now is to yield... I understand that."

The question remains, of course, whether yielding will be enough for Negan, or whether that's Rick's real plan. •

"YOU RULED THE ROOST, YOU BUILT SOMETHING, YOU THOUGHT YOU WERE SAFE, I GET IT... BUT THE WORD IS OUT, YOU ARE NOT SAFE... NOT EVEN CLOSE." **NEGAN**

"I HATE TO SAY IT, BUT IT'S ME OR YOU... AND WHENEVER THAT'S THE SITUATION, IT'S VERY EASY TO CHOOSE ME. NO OFFENSE." **CHRIS**

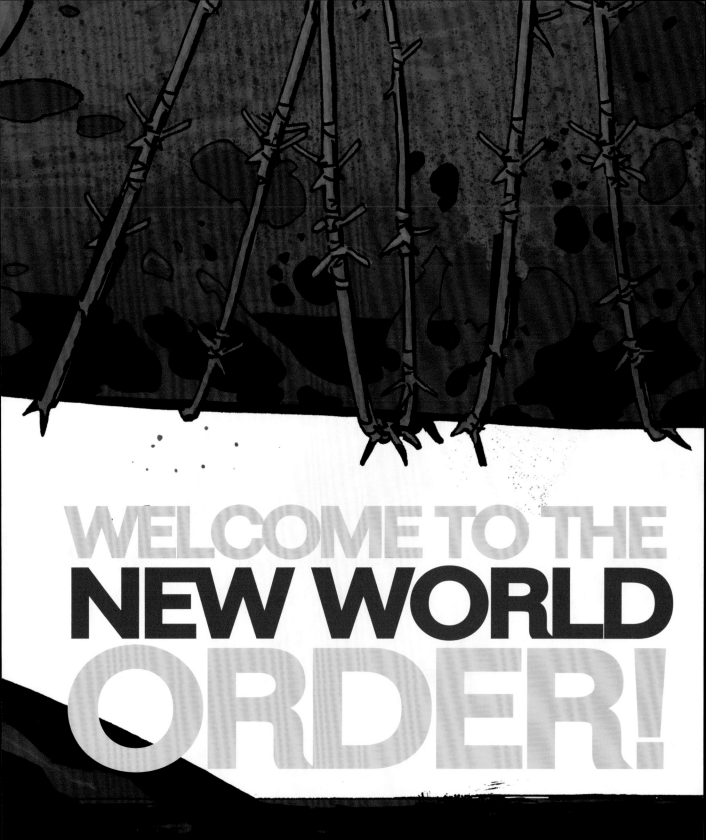

WELCOME TO THE NEW WORLD ORDER!

He wields a barbed baseball bat called Lucille, he leads a large group of warriors called The Saviors, and he is creating the world to his order. And Negan is his name-o... WORDS: Dan Auty

SEND WORD TO NEGAN. REPORT TO EVERYONE AT THEIR POSTS, TELL THEM TO GET IN POSITION.

WE ATTACK AT *DAWN.*

As anyone who has read more than a couple of issues of *The Walking Dead* will tell you, the zombies are not the real villains in the story. Sure, they represent a constant threat and inform almost every decision that Rick and those under his command make regarding their ongoing survival. But walkers are mindless creatures, relatively easy to deal with in smaller groups and easy to outwit. As long as you can ensure they don't get too close, you'll be OK.

The sad fact is that the true bad guys of *The Walking Dead* are *other people*. Throughout the course of more than 100 issues, Rick and company have faced all the deceit, mistrust, hatred, sadism and murderous intent that humanity has to offer; emotions and motivations that are usually kept beneath the surface of civilized society have emerged in all their ugly glory now that order has broken down. Previously good people have found their own morality tested by the extreme surroundings, while strong-willed individuals who always walked a fine line between right and wrong have taken advantage of the world's collapse to exert their own questionable authority.

ROTTEN APPLES

Into this latter group fall such characters as Dexter, Chris, the cannibalistic leader of the Hunters, and, of course, The Governor. But in the last few issues, a new villainous force has been introduced, one that promises to be the biggest single human threat that Rick and his people have yet faced. This is Negan, the enigmatic leader of the Saviors, a brutal group of survivors who, when we first hear of them in issue 96, are holding the potential sanctuary of the Hilltop community ransom.

The Saviors have struck a 'deal' with the dwellers of this farming community – half of everything they harvest, in return for keeping the hillsides free of walkers. The group upholds the deal via threats of violence, leading to an atmosphere of fear among the otherwise peaceful residents of Hilltop. Rick strikes a counter-agreement with their leader, Gregory – they will remove the threat of Negan and his men in return for desperately needed supplies. And so our heroes are put into direct conflict with Negan, and what they originally saw as a routine task of scaring away some less experienced survivors becomes something as dangerous and life-changing as anything they have faced so far.

What sets Negan apart from previous *Walking Dead* bad guys lies partly in the way that Robert Kirkman chooses to introduce him. Unlike The Governor – who suddenly appears in issue 27 and almost immediately establishes himself as a charismatic but cruel

"We are all Negan. He speaks through us and we speak for him. His words are ours." The Saviors

THIS PAGE The Saviors plan an ill-conceived attack on the Alexandria Safe-Zone. TOP RIGHT Initially, the Saviors seem nothing more than bullies, but... BOTTOM RIGHT Rick will learn to his cost that Negan has the numbers to cause a big problem.

despot – there is a slow, increasingly ominous build to Negan's eventual debut in issue 100.

WHAT'S IN A NAME?

At first, it's just a name – another leader of another gang taking what he can. No different from The Governor, Chris or even Rick himself.

Over the months, Rick's group has built itself into an impressively self-sufficient unit, relying on a formidable mix of brains and brawn, leading to an almost arrogant belief that they can deal with any foe that crosses their path. "I've dealt with his kind before," Rick tells Gregory. "We know how to handle people like that." Later on, when he returns to Alexandria, he describes

I LOVE LUCILLE!

Negan's barbed wire-encased club has already made an impression – mostly on Glenn's skull – and we can be sure that it will be making future appearances in *The Walking Dead*. But who or what could this dastardly miscreant have named the baseball bat after?

I Love Lucy
Negan may have been a big fan of 1950s' sitcom star Lucille Ball. It is a base-*ball* bat, after all.

King of the Blues
Legendary bluesman BB King named his guitar Lucille. Perhaps Negan is a fan of the man who once sang, "Look out, baby, I'm in a dangerous mood…"

Please Come Back
Another R'n'B legend with a fondness for the name is Little Richard who scored a 1957 hit with the song 'Lucille.' That said, it's a shame Negan didn't opt for a different Little Richard song and called his bat 'Tutti Frutti' instead.

> **"None of us have ever actually seen Negan. We didn't even know he was a real guy!" Gregory**

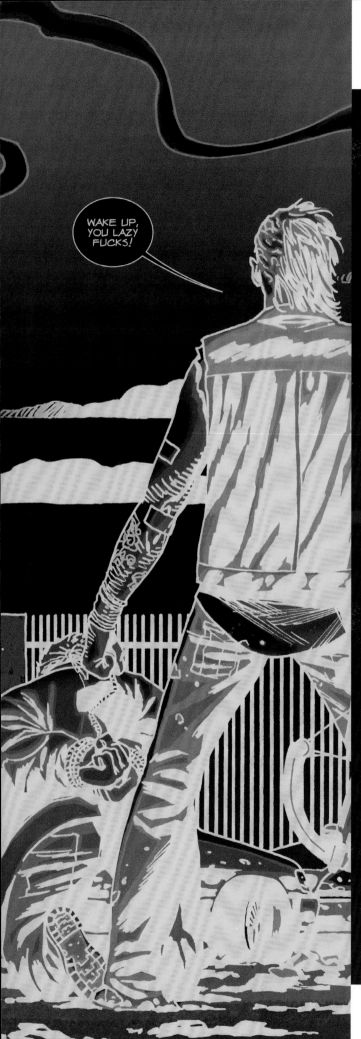

WAKE UP, YOU LAZY FUCKS!

ANYONE MOVES... AT ALL...

CUT THE BOY'S OTHER FUCKING EYE OUT AND FEED IT TO THE GIRL.

"The New World Order is this, and it's very simple. Give me your shit or I will kill you." Negan

Negan's threat as "a lot of hot air."

The first suggestion that Negan is a different type of adversary comes when the group encounters a quartet of Saviors for the first time, on their way back to Alexandria from negotiations at the Hilltop community. It's not that they look different from any other bunch of mean, tough road-warriors – but the way they refer to their as-yet-unseen leader implies a very different relationship to, say, that of The Governor and his men. In that case,

THAKK!

The Governor used lies and secrecy to rule over Woodbury and command respect among his men. Much of his power came from convincing those under him that he was a reasonable man, and it was those who opposed him who were the dangerous maniacs.

The Saviors are under no such misapprehension about Negan's intentions. And yet they do not seem to fear him – they speak of their leader more like members of a cult might, with respect and devotion. "We are all Negan. He speaks through us and we speak for him. His words are ours."

KRAKK!

The demise of Glenn at the hands of Negan and Lucille in issue 100 must rank as one of the most shocking and brutal killings in the entire comic book series.

YOU BUNCH OF PUSSIES... I'M JUST GETTING STARTED. LUCILLE IS THIRSTY.

FURTHER AND FERVOR

This is what makes the Saviors such a threat to both the residents of the Hilltop community and Rick's people – as history has proved time and time again, fanatical, blind obedience to a charismatic leader is a dangerous thing.

There is a solidarity implied among the Saviors. Of course, this is just another type of psychological manipulation, no different in many ways than using fear to command subservience, but it does

NEGAN VS THE GOVERNOR – WHO'S THE BADDEST?

The Governor was *The Walking Dead*'s number one bad guy for many issues, and still remains the book's premier villain for many. But Negan is the new kid on the block, and he has given The Governor a definite run for his money. But who is the most villainous character?

EVIL FACIAL HAIR

Negan may be cruel and ruthless, but without some top-lip foliage, his career as a murderous tyrant is going to flounder. Must do better. 1/10
The Governor understands that every great villain must possess distinctive facial hair, and sports a particularly cruel-looking mustache that screams 'evil'! 9/10

WEAPON OF CHOICE

Not one for guns or explosives, Negan strikes sadistic fear into the heart of his enemies with a barbed club he calls Lucille. 8/10
The Governor doesn't stick to one weapon – if it's handy, he'll use it. Demonstrates a wide skill set, but lacks the violent focus of Negan and his 'happy' stick. 6/10

WICKED WORDS

Negan can certainly talk – his first appearance is a long, rambling monologue about what he does and what he plans to do. But he says it with a smile and clearly has a sense of humor – maybe we will discover that he was a stand-up comedian in his pre-apocalypse life. 7/10
The Governor is a less eloquent orator, and does perhaps get to the point quicker. There are few lines as chilling as, "I plan on doing this every day as often as I can, until you figure out some way to kill yourself!" A tie then. 7/10

WHAT'S IN A NAME?

A good villain needs a scary name, and Negan is certainly a strange, distinctive moniker. Let's just hope we don't find out his full name is Nigel Negan or something. 8/10
The Governor is a cool name. Shame that his real one – Brian – is so unthreatening that he had to steal his brother Philip's identity before adopting a more officious title. But then, is Philip any scarier? 5/10

FINAL SCORE

The Governor just edges this fight, largely due to Negan's disappointing performance in the mustache department. But a few days off from shaving and we might have a different story…

"I thought we could handle these 'Saviors'. I was wrong. A conflict with this group could result in the death of us all." Rick

OH, GOD...

...GLENN.

Rick and Maggie are helpless to stop the death of Glenn. Negan improves his batting average.

suggest that these men will fight to the bitter end for their master. And when the Saviors bring the conflict to Rick's doorstep in issue 98 – resulting in deaths on both sides – there is the suggestion that they have acted on their own initiative, without Negan's direct command, just an implicit understanding of what he would expect from them.

Negan's decision to keep himself from those he is oppressing only serves to create an air of fearsome mystery among those he seeks to exploit. He hasn't even revealed himself to the Hilltop community, using his followers as his mouthpiece. Gregory is astonished when he learns that Negan came out of hiding to confront Rick: "None of us have ever actually seen Negan. We didn't even know he was a real guy!"

Rick may have been expecting just another weak tyrant, but Kirkman's masterful build-up to his eventual appearance implies otherwise. There was no way the writer would spend four issues teasing the reader with Negan's name without delivering something more than just another ordinary bad guy. Of course, he *is* just a man, but his very first scene sees Rick and those unlucky enough to have been traveling with him when they were ambushed at a distinct disadvantage. Surrounded by Saviors, Negan lays down the law: "The New World Order is this, and it's very simple. Give me your shit or I will kill you."

THE HORROR, THE HORROR
What we learn of Negan in this relatively brief encounter seems to be a man defined by contradiction. He is verbose but foul-mouthed – Negan has a lot to say, all of it supported by

a stream of inventive swearing. He is unquestionably savage – the brutal slaying of Glenn in front of his friends and the mother of his unborn child confirms this. But while Negan's face reveals a sadistic pleasure in the murder, he also tells the group that he does not want to kill any of them – the fewer of them there are, the fewer supplies can be gathered for him. Glenn's murder is purely a demonstration of his will and as an act of justice for the men that he lost to Rick.

Most curiously, considering he is responsible for one of the most shocking killings in the series, he seems unusually bothered about how his choice of victim would be perceived by others. He initially dismisses Heath, Michonne, and Glenn because of their skin color – "I'm a lot of things but I'd never want to be called a racist. You're off limits." – and in the end he selects randomly, ensuring that no one of his potential victims gets "special" treatment.

And that's it... for now. With a final reiteration that Negan is now in control of their lives, he disappears with his men into the night, leaving a badly shaken group far less sure of their place in the world than before. As we see in the next few issues, this devastating encounter with Negan causes Rick to question his very approach to those who wish to abuse and oppress. Would a less aggressive approach to the problem of the Saviors have kept Glenn alive?

A relationship with the Hilltop community that once seemed filled with the promise of safety is now fraught with danger and uncertainty. Only one thing is guaranteed – we haven't seen the last of Negan... •

CLASH OF THE TITANS

'End Trails' takes a closer look at the best confrontations between characters. This time, it's Rick versus Negan in the build up to 'All Out War.' **WORDS: Dan Auty**

WHAT'S THE BEEF?

A confrontation between Rick and Negan had been brewing since issue 100, when the latter brutally murdered Glenn. Things come to a head when Rick discovers that Negan has killed Spencer, breaking an agreement that Negan wouldn't touch any of Rick's people if they kept the Saviors in supplies.

ROUND ONE!

Rick is quick to round on Negan, demanding that he explain his actions, warning that he will not leave the Alexandria Safe-Zone alive if he refuses. The determined, steely look in Rick's eyes shows that he is not kidding – it will take more than a baseball bat with a dumb name to scare him.

ROUND TWO!

On the face of it, Negan's response is measured. He expresses indignation that Rick doesn't realize how reasonable he has been for not killing Carl when the kid shot at him. He even offers to let Rick keep their supplies as a peace offering. Is Negan going soft?

ROUND THREE!

Seeing an opportunity, Rick races to Andrea, telling her to scale the church tower with her rifle and take out Negan and his men. As the bullets start flying, Negan's soldiers drop like flies and Rick prepares to execute his nemesis.

THE DECIDING BLOW

Unfortunately, Negan is not an idiot. A fully armed back-up team quickly disarm Rick's men, turning the advantage back to Negan.

AND THE WINNER IS…

As the issue closes, things look very, very bad for Rick. Or as Negan says in his usual eloquent manner: "You're fucking fucked, you stupid fucker."

And so the war begins… •

THE SECRET DIARY OF A WALKER

It's not easy being a zombie in *The Walking Dead* world, as our week in the life/death of an undead walker shows. Diary entries transcribed by Dan Auty…

Monday

A quiet day – went for a stroll in the woods to take in some natural air. I'm not saying I smell nice, but my pals absolutely reek. Good job they're only interested in intestines

these days, because there's no way they'd meet a nice undead girl stinking like that.

Tuesday

Jon came to visit. Told me a bunch of normos had been hanging round and asked if I'd like to get a bite to eat. I was tempted but I've been trying a new diet, sticking to berries and squirrels. Jon gave me a funny look, but that might be because his eye is halfway down his cheek.

Wednesday

Getting bored of this wood. It poured with rain last night, the squirrels keep running up trees and the berries go right through

me. Literally, since my stomach fell out – along with my other organs – three weeks ago.

Thursday

Things got a lot more interesting today! Those normos showed up. They were playing a very odd game – first this girl hung herself from a tree, then the men pointed guns at each other, then the girl woke up and everyone hugged. I just couldn't get the hang of the rules at all…

Friday

Was awoken very rudely by one of the normos urinating in a bush – the one I was sleeping under! Naturally, I got drenched in the foul-smelling stuff! I was outraged and almost vomited on the spot! I'm positive he did it on purpose. Anyway, between the squirrels, berries and this, I'd had enough. I was about to tell this a-hole what I thought of him, when his buddy turned up with a gun. Now I've got a killer headache, too! •

COMING OF AGE
THE LIFE & TIMES OF CARL GRIMES

NO BOOK ABOUT *THE WALKING DEAD* WOULD BE COMPLETE WITHOUT A SPECIAL FEATURE ON THE SERIES' LEADING YOUNG CHARACTER: CARL GRIMES. OVER THE NEXT FEW PAGES, *TWDM* TAKES AN IN-DEPTH LOOK AT THE HEROIC YOUNG PROTAGONIST, FROM SMALL BOY TO WORLD-WEARY TEEN.

WORDS: RUSSELL COOK

"Carl is the guy who killed Shane and who has done things he's never going to forget," Robert Kirkman told *TWDM* in issue# 11. Those are words that are rarely used to describe a child; they make young Master Grimes sound like a man way beyond his own years. And that's what makes our diminutive hero such an interesting, albeit tragic, character.

Since his first appearance as a seven-year old boy in issue #2 of the comic, Carl Grimes has changed profoundly (and not just physically). Back then, despite the rise of the undead, he appeared to feel safe; his sheriff father and doting mother kept him well protected. Nevertheless, even in those early days, he showed an awareness of his surroundings that belied his young age. As the zombies kept on coming, he knew he had to learn how to use a gun because he knew he would need one at some point in the future.

But still, kids are small – an obvious, yet undeniable fact – meaning Carl was no match for a hungry walker in those early days. As such, he watched the likes of Shane, Glenn and his father, looking to them as a means of defending himself. Yet, throughout his development, Carl's persona has become utterly unique in the group. He has shown glimpses of being a 'Grimes,' but he has gradually become his own man, seemingly taking the best bits of Rick and, at times, casting aside the worst.

CARL APPEARS TO HAVE NO PROBLEM WITH MAKING THE CALL TO KILL ANOTHER HUMAN BEING IF THAT PERSON SEEMS LIKE A THREAT TO THE GROUP.

GIVING IT BOTH BARRELS

It wasn't long before Carl put his firearms training to good use; firstly to protect his mom from a walker and, secondly, to protect his father from Shane, who in a state of rage, drew a gun on Rick. This left Carl with no choice but to put the crazed fool down with a shot to the

WHEN THE GOVERNOR ENACTED HIS BRUTAL ATTACK ON THE PRISON, RESULTING IN THE DEATH OF JUDITH AND LORI, CARL'S CHILDHOOD WAS OVER.

IT DIDN'T SCARE ME. I *WANTED* YOU TO DO THAT... I WANTED TO *HELP.*

I HAVE THOUGHTS...

I'M SCARED IF YOU KNEW THE THOUGHTS I HAD SOMETIMES THAT YOU'D *HATE* ME...

neck. "It's not the same as killing the dead ones, Daddy," he says afterwards, showing mature awareness of what he had just done.

Rick responds with some fatherly advice, saying, "It never should be son. It never should be."

This moment is the first indication of a key difference between Papa and Baby Grimes: Carl appears to have no problem with making the call to kill another human being if that person seems like a threat to the group, while Rick has nearly always struggled with it.

Shortly after killing Shane, Carl feels what it's like to be on the other end of the firing line, when Otis inadvertently shoots him. Thankfully, due to the veterinarian magic of Hershel Greene, he survives. While this appeared to do little more than superficial physical damage to Carl, it's obvious, in hindsight, that this was a contributing factor to the steely, fearless attitude of the adolescent Mr Grimes we know today.

STAY BACK!

BIG BROTHER

Most people fear being locked up, but after getting shot, and eventually being forced to leave Hershel Greene's farm, Carl and the group stumble across the prison. For the first time, they have a place where they feel safe. It has fences, watchtowers, showers and even land where they could grow crops.

It was here where Carl's maturation was accelerated; during Rick's prolonged absence at Woodbury, Carl took on the mantle of protector, looking after his pregnant mom. He reassured Lori that Rick would return safely with an assuredness that was startling for a boy who, by that point, had already seen first-hand more death than many a soldier

on the frontline. He also offered Sophia a shoulder to cry on after her mother, Carol, died. He's one tough cookie, our Carl.

The subsequent birth of his baby sister, Judith, brought much-needed joy to the Grimes family and the group of survivors in general, but her coming into the world also presented a new challenge that Carl was more than willing to take on. He was protective of her in the same way Rick was of him. When the Governor enacted his brutal attack on the prison, resulting in the death of both Judith and Lori, Carl hit a real turning point: his childhood was over.

THE SHOE'S ON THE OTHER FOOT

After fleeing the carnage at the prison with his father, the importance of Carl's character as a plot device became explicitly apparent. It was at this point that he became an embodiment of Rick's major weakness: the desire to protect those he loves, no matter

THERE'S BEEN A WORRYING DEVELOPMENT IN CARL, A LACK OF EMPATHY TOWARDS ALL BUT THE CLOSEST OF FRIENDS.

what the cost may be. But, Carl also became a symbolic representation of Rick's biggest strength: the fearless ability to help others and bring out their survival skills in the face of adversity.

This manifests itself when Rick begins to lose his mind: convinced he was speaking to his dead wife on the telephone, he somehow forgot what death meant. Carl was left with no choice but to fight and protect his dad, despite feeling anger towards him for some of the decisions he had made in the past.

This was where we started to see a dividing line between father and son. Carl thought some things should have been handled differently, and ultimately blamed his father for the death of his mother and sister.

It wasn't until Carl and Rick, along with Abraham, were held at knifepoint by bandits that order was somewhat restored. Incapacitating Rick, the nasty animals set about sexually assaulting our young hero; his need for protection surfaced for the first time in a long period. Thankfully, it was just the tonic Rick needed to revive his will to live. He broke free by biting the neck of one his captors, before killing all three of the scumbags with help from his new friend Abraham.

This was a pivotal moment, both in terms of the story and to stop Rick from being overly protective, almost second-guessing himself at every turn, and take back his rightful role as a proactive leader.

I'M SCARED... BUT YOU CAN'T TELL. CAN YOU?

CARL'S DECISION-MAKING SEEMS TO BE VERY MUCH BLACK AND WHITE, WITH LITTLE CONCEPT OF ANY MORALLY GRAY AREAS.

A NEW LAW

Rick's steely determination and resilience in the face of danger is something that has clearly been passed on to his son, especially when it comes to protecting those they love. But it's been matched by a worrying development in Carl, a lack of empathy towards all but the closest of friends.

The first evidence of this was when Carl made a decision to execute another young boy, Ben, who had misunderstood the difference between dead and undead and killed his own twin brother, Billy (issue #61). It was a childish mistake that Carl would never make. While the group deliberate over how best to deal with Ben – some were in favor of execution, others were horrified at the thought – Carl takes matters into his own hands. He sneaks into Ben's tent and shoots him dead –

I ONLY WANT NEGAN. HE KILLED MY FRIEND.

TURN HIM OVER TO ME, AND I'LL LET THE REST OF YOU LIVE. I'VE SEEN THE WEAPONS YOU USE, I KNOW YOU DON'T HAVE A LOT OF GUNS.

NO ONE ELSE NEEDS TO DIE.

CARL HAS THE POTENTIAL TO BECOME A COMMUNITY LEADER IN THE FUTURE. IF ONLY HE CAN GET HIS ANGER UNDER CONTROL.

immediacy and lack of thought for others shows a recklessness that only comes with youth. He stowed away in one of Negan's trucks with the intention of assassinating the tyrant, arming himself with an automatic rifle bigger than him. It was a bold but stupid move: his inevitable failed attempt and capture left him, his father and the rest of the Alexandrians in a precarious position.

Nevertheless, Carl's actions were well intentioned at least, and do show that he has the potential to become a community leader in the future. If only he can get his anger under control. Perhaps you can blame the Negan incident on

perhaps taking his father's earlier edict of "You kill, you die" a little too literally.

This moment shows a level of maturity, but is deliberately problematic too. Ben certainly had to be dealt with, and while the adults hesitated because of his age, Carl had no such qualms. But equally, Carl's decision-making seems to be very much black and white, with little concept of any morally gray areas.

This coldness becomes even more evident after Carl is shot for the second time. A brief respite is given when the survivors reach the relative safety of Alexandria, and Carl is allowed to play with the other kids in the encampment. When the Safe-Zone is overrun by a herd of walkers, Douglas Monroe accidentally shoots Carl in the head, taking out one of his eyes. Thankfully, the little fella wakes up a few issues later, but since that point Carl has become more morally detached than ever. Anger seems to be the driving force behind most of his actions.

After Glenn's brutal death at the hands of Negan in issue #100, Carl's thirst for revenge is seemingly much greater than Rick's. Negan must die for what he did, Carl decided, and if Rick wasn't going to do it, then he most certainly would. As readers, we know that that wasn't the case – Rick was simply playing a longer game – but Carl's

raging hormones – he is still a teenager after all – but there's definitely potential there for leadership.

The question of whether Carl could one day lead the group still hangs in the air. He is often too easily led by his negative emotions and acts before thinking things through properly. If he manages to control these, then there's no reason why he couldn't step into Rick's shoes in the future.

WHAT THE FUTURE HOLDS

From this point on, Carl becomes more central to the narrative than ever before and, since then, he has helped shape its trajectory. After the events of

AFTER ALL THE HARDSHIP, PHYSICAL AND EMOTIONAL PAIN CARL'S BEEN THROUGH, IT'S BEEN GOOD TO SEE A MORALISTIC ADULT BEGINNING TO EMERGE.

'All Out War' and the time-jump, Carl seems to have settled down a little bit. He has also become a lot more emotionally engaged with those around him, finding both a best friend, Josh, and a girlfriend, Lydia. He also has a new job – a blacksmith's apprentice at the Hilltop – that gives him a sense of pride and duty. All give him a reason to live – no more running off on solo assassination attempts.

After all the hardship, physical and emotional pain Carl's been through, not to mention a lack of a real childhood, it has been good to see signs of a moralistic and very humane adult beginning to emerge from the cold-hearted boy we knew pre-'All Out War.' For a figure with very few happy memories, it is important for Carl as a character, and as a figure for the readers to identify with, that this happens. It provides hope and something to

hold onto amid the relentless trauma and misery that abounds in *The Walking Dead*.

His growing relationship with Lydia is a huge step forward, despite her being a former prisoner and a member of the Whisperers. We are beginning to witness Carl grow up and, as a plot device, it's evidence of a shift towards a maturity that matches his father's. His rage is still a problem at times – he beats Sophia's bullies almost to death, for instance, when he has the skills to merely incapacitate them – but he's also shown he's one of the most valued members of the community: a fearless combatant who has begun to understand what is needed to do more than just survive.

It will be interesting to see how Carl reacts to Alpha's killing of Josh and his other friends: will we see the old Carl re-emerge, or the new, more thoughtful Carl take action?

Time will tell... •

THE SORRY SAGA

WHAT ARE YOU THINKING ABOUT?

WHAT?

WE WERE TALKING ABOUT ATLANTA--WHEN I FIRST SHOWED UP AT THE CAMP. THEN YOU ZONED OUT.

WHAT ARE YOU THINKING ABOUT?

OF LORI GRIMES

When it comes to shocking moments in *The Walking Dead* mythos, the death of Lori Grimes (in both the comic and AMC's TV series) would surely top most fans' list. Her demise left a big space in the lives of those around her: while her husband Rick is most certainly the leader of the Atlanta survivors, Lori was their heart, as *TWDM* discovers in this review of her life post-apocalypse. WORDS: Dan Auty

"RICK AND I ARE THE MOST COMPATIBLE PEOPLE ON EARTH. WE ARE PERFECT FOR EACH OTHER."
VOLUME ONE: DAYS GONE BY

It's fair to say that no character in *The Walking Dead* has had it easy. Simply surviving in this harsh, dangerous world is a struggle in itself, and many have had to endure previously unimaginable hardship in order to stay alive. But few of Robert Kirkman's creations have had quite as miserable a time as Lori Grimes. Her position as Rick's wife has frequently put her in a difficult position as regards both her husband and the others in the group. But while her previous role as a suburban housewife may have provided few practical skills with which to deal with a world overrun by zombies, there is one job to which she is completely and utterly dedicated – keeping her family alive.

Lori's introduction in both the comic and on the TV show is much the same. From the very start, she is thrown into a difficult situation from which there would clearly be no happy way out. Believing Rick is lying dead in hospital, Lori heads to Atlanta with their son Carl and

"THIS NEW BABY WILL NEVER KNOW WHAT THE WORLD WAS LIKE, HELL… CARL WON'T REALLY REMEMBER MUCH OF IT HIMSELF BEFORE TOO LONG." VOLUME TWO: MILES BEHIND US

a few issues, but the building tension between the three is no less pronounced. Lori's expression as she stands, rain-soaked at the end of issue three, telling Shane that it was a mistake, says it all, and establishes the mix of emotions that is to mark her throughout the rest of her time in the comic. Namely, pain, pity and regret. By the time Shane lies dead in the ground, a steely defiance has descended upon her. "You son of a bitch," she snarls, spitting on his grave.

In the TV show, the effect of Lori's liaison with Shane is more slowly played out, and indeed more insidious. Over the course of the first two seasons, the guilt weighs heavily upon her – even when she confesses all to Rick in season two's 'Triggerfinger,' it does little to stem the deterioration of their relationship.

Lori comes to realize how little she actually knows about many of those closest to her. "You're not a killer," she tells

Rick's best friend and police colleague Shane Walsh, where a group slowly forms among the survivors there. Lonely and overcome with grief, Lori begins a relationship with Shane, who settles very comfortably into his role as both her lover and father figure to Carl.

Of course, Rick's sudden arrival at their woodland camp throws the situation into chaos: Lori's joy at her husband's survival is matched by the guilt she feels about her dalliance with Shane.

OUT, DAMNED SPOT! OUT, I SAY!
It was through her relationships with Shane and Rick that we first get to know Lori. In the comic book, Shane is around for only

Rick early on in season three, but she knows she is wrong. Rick has stepped up to that role very well. The killing of Shane – not to mention the involvement of her son in this act – in issue six (comic) and 'Better Angels' (TV, season two) and his uncompromising leadership of the group may all be in the service of keeping them alive, but it removes any last hope that the man she married might return.

MOM'S THE WORD
Much of the reason, especially in the show, that Lori's relationship with those around her suffers is that she puts every bit of herself

PUTTING THE 'SELF' IN SELFLESS

It would be a mistake, however, to think purely of Lori as a conflicted wife and struggling mother. In the early issues of the comic, she proves herself to be a valuable, self-sufficient member of the group, inspiring a sense of purpose among her female compatriots. When some in the group – Donna in particular – question why the women are expected to clean clothes while the men kill zombies and gather

"WHAT IS IT ABOUT OUR SITUATION THAT MAKES YOU ASSUME THE BEST IN PEOPLE?" VOLUME THREE: SAFETY BEHIND BARS

into her responsibilities as a mother. The speed at which boys grow is bewildering at the best of times, but when they are learning to survive in a zombie-infested wasteland, a once-loving relationship becomes badly strained. One result of Carl shooting Shane to protect his dad (killing him outright in the comic and as a zombie in the show) is that it brings him closer to Rick; almost inevitably his strong, authoritative father becomes a far more powerful role model than his mother.

Carl is desperate to step up and prove himself a 'man,' whether it's searching for lost Sophia in the woods around Hershel's farm or clearing the prison of walkers; this regularly puts him at odds with Lori, who wants to protect him both physically and psychologically. Lori is forced to question her abilities as a parent; "I'm not winning any mother of the year awards," she tells Rick in the show – his assurances otherwise do little to change her opinion. Only at the very end does she reassert herself as Carl's devoted guardian.

supplies, Lori quickly grasps the reality of the situation: "I can't shoot a gun, and I've never even tried. And I wouldn't trust any of those guys to wash my clothes. This isn't about women's rights."

Throughout the course of nearly 50 issues and 23 episodes, Lori remains one of the least selfish members of the group, cutting through the bullshit and ego that sometimes leads others to make rash decisions. She was the only one to raise any objection to letting the prisoners live among them when the group first reached the prison in the comic, while on the TV show had her warnings to Rick about Shane been heeded earlier, then much trouble might have been avoided. "Shane thinks I'm his... and he thinks you can't protect us. He's dangerous and he won't stop," she cautions Rick towards the end of season two.

A FRIEND IN NEED...

Inevitably, however, Lori's empathetic nature also leads her to attract the attention of some of the group's neediest members. In the comic, her close friendship with Carol becomes strained as the other woman starts to behave in an increasingly erratic manner after the group arrives at the prison. But with the others uninterested in the situation and with Carol's bizarre 'marriage' proposal as the final straw, Lori takes the unusual step of shutting her out. Carol's subsequent suicide

"WE'VE GOT A CHANCE TO CHANGE THINGS, RICK. WE'VE GOT A CHANCE TO BREAK THE CYCLE. 'NO KILLING' MEANS NO KILLING." VOLUME THREE: SAFETY BEHIND BARS

weighs heavily on her, and Lori takes on the additional responsibility of becoming Sophia's guardian.

In both mediums, Lori falls pregnant with a child that may or may not be Rick's. In the comic, it is her husband she tells first; on the show, Glenn discovers the truth when Lori sends him to pick up a pregnancy test while making a run to a nearby pharmacy.

But in both cases, Lori has no choice but to continue as normal. In the show, she considers inducing a miscarriage, but throws the pills up almost straight away; in the comic it is never even discussed.

The big difference between the two mediums is that in the show Shane is still alive when Rick learns about the pregnancy; if there's any one event that drives the final wedge between these former friends, it is when Shane realizes that Lori will never allow him to have anything to do with the child. "Even if it's yours, it's not gonna be yours," she tells him. "And there's nothing you can do to change that."

THIS IS THE END

Lori does get to experience being a mother for a second time in the comic; for a few issues, Judith's arrival and the apparent safety of

the prison bring a new purpose into Lori's life. She and Rick are brought closer together, while Carl loves having a little sister. But all this comes to a horrifying end in issue 48, when both Lori and Judith are shot dead during The Governor's final assault on the prison. This is one of, if not *the* most shocking moments in the whole series – provocative in both the graphic depiction of their death and in the sudden way in which it arrives.

On TV, Lori's demise in 'Killer Within' in season three is no less powerful, but perhaps a little more expected. A sense of finality hangs over her during her final few episodes, as if she is trying to

COME HERE, CARL.

"IT'S NOT THAT I CARE LESS ABOUT RICK, IT'S NOT THAT AT ALL. IT'S JUST HE ALWAYS COMES BACK. AT THIS POINT, I'D BE MORE SURPRISED IF HE DIDN'T RETURN." VOLUME SIX: THIS SORROWFUL LIFE

OH, NOTHING. JUST...

DWELLING.

WE'VE BEEN THROUGH A LOT THESE PAST MONTHS. I WAS JUST THINKING ABOUT IT ALL...

head. Although in general the comic book plunges into darker places than the TV show, in many ways Lori's time onscreen was harder – her death more protracted, without the joy of ever holding her baby or knowing that her husband still loved her.

IT'S A SAD, SAD, SAD, SAD WORLD

Rick and Carl's reactions to Lori's death are very different between comic and show, largely due to their respective circumstances.

On the page, Lori is killed as what remains of the group flee the prison. Her husband and son have little time to grieve before they are back out on the road, fighting to survive.

In the show, the group are still together and so are able to offer support in the wake of Lori's death. For Rick, the regret he feels at losing Lori while still on bad terms manifests itself as a series of hallucinations. He ends up saying his true goodbye to a disembodied voice on the end of a long-dead telephone, although it isn't until the season finale when he finally lets her go. Carl continues to grow up very quickly, with a haunted determination – there is the sense that he has seen so much death in his few years on the planet that while his mother's passing pains him, in the end she is just another dead loved one in a long line of dead loved ones.

It would be a mistake to see Lori as a passive character, and even though her death was important narratively, both mediums seem strangely empty without her. Her life was not a happy one, but her influence on two of the series' most important male characters was profound, and provided much of the heart that makes *The Walking Dead* so powerful. •

reconcile with both Rick and Carl before her end. In the event, she dies while giving birth, with Maggie forced to perform an emergency C-section in a squalid prison boiler room.

In perhaps the show's most moving scene to date, Lori bids a heart-rending farewell to Carl, before her son puts a bullet in her

CARL GRIMES

'Choice Cuts' takes a closer look at a specific character in *The Walking Dead*. This time, young Carl Grimes is the focus, as we select his brightest moments, his darkest hours, and his, well, choicest cuts from both the comic book and TV series.

WORDS: Russell Cook

SPOILER ALERT: IF YOU'RE NOT UP TO DATE, THIS FEATURE CONTAINS POTENTIAL SPOILER CONTENT FOR BOTH THE COMIC AND TV SERIES

FIRST APPEARANCE

The Walking Dead reveals many things about humanity's unpredictable and often violent reaction to being placed under immense pressure. But perhaps its most powerful exposé of our response to life-shattering upheaval is its exploration of the fragility of innocence, embodied by young Carl.

Rick and Lori's son made his first appearance in issue two of the comic series, when Rick, previously assumed dead, arrived at the group's camp on the fringes of a heavily infested Atlanta. Having been whisked off there by his dad's best-pal-gone-bad, Shane Walsh, Carl did not expect to see Rick again. His emotive return to the family marks Carl's first highlight of the series, and is one of just a few high points not to be immediately followed by a bloodbath.

CARL FACT FILE

NAME: Carl Grimes

PLAYED BY: Chandler Riggs

AGE: Seven to nine (comic); 13 (TV)

JOB: Kid

FAMILY: Father (Rick), Mother (Lori – deceased), sister (Judith – deceased [comic]/ alive [TV])

RELATIONSHIPS POST-APOCALYPSE: Sophia

LIKES: Rick, Lori, Sophia, Michonne, Andrea

DISLIKES: The Governor, Negan, green beans

FIRST APPEARANCE: Issue two (comics); Season one, episode one: 'Days Gone By' (TV)

CURRENT STATUS: Alive in both comic and TV show

THE SECOND AMENDMENT

Even at just seven years old, Carl had an obvious desire to muck in and do his bit, so, when Rick suggested showing him how to use a gun, his excitement was palpable. With the growing dangers that surrounded the group, putting a gun in the hands of his young son showed real forethought (and perhaps a little craziness) on the part of Rick; but the act also helped to establish the first real dividing line between him and Lori.

Nonetheless, Carl's natural shooting ability was undeniable; when he asked whether he could "carry a gun like everyone else," Rick wasn't really left with a choice, meaning he could only say yes to the excitable starry-eyed boy.

In a world where the dead were roaming free and the human mind was being pushed to its limits, arming his son proved to be one of the best decisions Rick ever made. For Carl, the gesture was a significant turning point and one of the many incremental moments that helped to shape him into the fearless warrior he has eventually become.

"DON'T HURT MY DADDY AGAIN!"

When he came to the rescue of his father, a blubbering Carl experienced the true power of holding a firearm. Held at gunpoint by his former best pal Shane, Rick was seconds from death, but young Carl stepped up and did what had to be done, putting one between the eyes of his dad's former policing partner.

That moment – occurring much later in the TV adaptation, albeit with an undead Shane (season two's 'Better Angels') – represents both a highlight and lowlight for Carl. His bravery, fearlessness and indecision saved his father's life, and this quick introduction to the value of looking after your own proved to be a useful lesson.

But the reality of killing someone also changed him forever. The father-son bond might have been strengthened by that terrible deed, but the all-important roles of protector and protected were turned on their head, paving the way for later issues between the two.

"DOES THIS MEAN I GET TO CARRY A GUN NOW LIKE EVERYONE ELSE?"
VOLUME ONE: DAYS GONE BY

BACK PAIN

In issue nine, Rick and Tyreese leave the group in search of food and a place for them to stay, but not before Carl was able to make his claim for being involved, saying, "I can help. I shoot real good." Rick was placed in a difficult situation: Carl had saved his life, so, despite being the boy's father, who was he to tell him otherwise?

Out of nowhere, as the three of them searched

tirelessly, a shot was fired that hit Carl in the back, immediately laying bare his vulnerability and innocence in one fell swoop.

The artwork reasserts that defenselessness, picturing him falling hard towards the ground. This painful event might have strengthened Carl in the long run, but it was nothing short of a low point for him, as once again his struggle for the respect of his elders was thrown into tatters.

"YOU TAKE CARE OF YOUR DADDY FOR ME, ALL RIGHT? YOU'RE GOING TO BE FINE. YOU'RE GOING TO BEAT THIS WORLD, I KNOW YOU WILL." LORI, SEASON THREE, 'KILLER WITHIN'

KISS IT BETTER

After initially resisting the playful efforts of Carol's daughter, Sophia, Carl, despite his young age, realized how, much like everybody else in that troublesome world, he needed somebody else to confide in and trust. He decided to take the little sweetheart up on her offer, saying, "I changed my mind. I'll be your boyfriend if you still want me to be. I think you're pretty and stuff."

To demonstrate their new understanding, Sophia planted a big sloppy kiss on Carl's cheek, and although it made the young lad squirm, it is one of the most human things he has experienced on his torrid journey to date. Of course, being kids, their love was a little naïve at first, but it was love nonetheless and theirs was a bond that became one of the few unshakeable relationships in the series, with their friendship extending its way throughout.

BITESIZE PIECES

When Rick, Abraham and Carl traveled back to Rick's old police station for supplies, they were accosted by a group of animalistic bandits who, albeit indirectly, and in the most terrible manner imaginable, restored the father-son bond at the center of *The Walking Dead*'s story.

As the men set about demolishing what little shred of innocence Carl had left, Rick and Abraham were forced to watch. But in a bloody and powerful last ditch effort, Rick, in a fashion that scarily resembled the undead, fought his way free by tearing a hunk of flesh out of his captors' throat with his teeth, before clambering up and lunging forward to save his son.

For the time being, their relationship was once again back on course, and while the whole event was a traumatic one for Carl, it strengthened his relationship with his father. It was a subtle highlight amid the brutal chaos of *The Walking Dead* world.

"I'M SCARED IF YOU KNEW THE THOUGHTS I HAD SOMETIMES THAT YOU'D HATE ME." CARL, VOLUME 10: WHAT WE BECOME

THE COURSE OF TRUE LOVE...

In stark contrast to the youthful love they enjoy in the comic, Carl and Sophia's friendship in the TV adaptation is unfortunately not so pleasant, with a conclusion that is a definite low point for the little hero.

After disappearing in episode one of season two, the group tirelessly searched for Sophia in every possible place imaginable, while Carl, still unconscious after being shot by Otis, was unable to help out. Despite his serious injuries, Carl woke up briefly to ask whether Sophia was OK. He clearly cared for Sophia, and as the two youngest in the group, they shared a special bond. So when the poor girl's tiny body emerged from Hershel's barn as one of the less-than-pretty roamers, Carl, much like everyone else, was left utterly heartbroken and collapsed into his mother's arms ('Pretty Much Dead Already').

But, it's not all doom and gloom... Oh, wait, yes it is. As so often in *The Walking Dead*, tragedy was followed by even more tragedy – somebody had to put a bullet in the little girl's head, and who else would step up to do it, but Carl's father Rick? As the sheriff raised his gun and pointed it at the little girl's head, Carl could do nothing but watch his poor friend's demise, marking yet another brutal tragedy in his less than pleasant adolescence.

EYE FOR AN EYE

Carl was dealt another physical blow in issue 83 of the comic series when he was accidentally shot in the head during a frenzied zombie fight. His dad's pleas for the group to stop their wild shooting were quickly cut short when he turned to see a bullet making its way through Carl's eye. Artist Charlie Adlard does a great job of creating the heart-stopping image that sums up another of Carl's lowest points in the series, but thankfully over the next 15 or so issues he slowly recovered and, having lost the sight in one eye, he became wilder, angrier and more ready than ever for life after a zombie apocalypse.

Carl might have taken a beating, but he has become more of a soldier for it (and in many ways more like the Carl of the TV show). Every shred of who Carl was before the apocalypse has been completely etched away; he has been forced to grow up much quicker than most children his age.

MOM!

Season three of *The Walking Dead* TV adaptation saw Carl's role within the group grow in stature. In light of falling numbers, a growing list of injuries, an ever-growing sense of hopelessness, and diminishing trust in his father's leadership, little Grimes stepped up to show his mettle. Wearing his father's sheriff hat, Carl was cooler, calmer – and colder. He was a straight-shooter and had become trusted enough to be left in charge of looking after the seemingly weaker members of the group at the prison.

However, there are some things nobody can be prepared for. When his mother Lori fell into labor, it became quickly apparent that she was unable to give birth naturally, and

after pleading with Maggie to perform a makeshift Caesarean, Carl had to stand by and witness the death of his mother. The worst was yet to come though. After his mother's passing, Carl had to decide whether to put a bullet in her head, or whether to leave her to turn. In one of the series' most powerful and heart-wrenching moments, a single shot was heard that has left Carl potentially beyond repair.

Lori's death is very different in the comic book, but arguably this moment as portrayed in the TV series is just as shocking, not just because it was so unexpected, but also because of some brilliant acting from Chandler Riggs and Sarah Wayne Callies.

GRIMES & MISDEMEANORS

After stowing away in one of brutal tyrant Negan's trucks, Carl took a stand in issue 104. Jumping out from underneath some canvases, he shot wildly at Negan's men, yelling, "I only want Negan. He killed my friend." Unfortunately for him, a child's body and the recoil on an assault rifle is not a happy mix. Still, he did manage to kill six of Negan's Saviors.

Doing what his father would not, he faced up to the blood-hungry maniac, but still showed some humanity when he told everyone else they need not die. Carl was there for one reason; to avenge his friend's death. Negan responded to Carl's demands, saying in typical fashion, "Kid, I'm not going to lie to you – you scare the fucking shit out of me."

> "KID, I'M NOT GOING TO LIE TO YOU – YOU SCARE ME."
> NEGAN, ISSUE 104

Right there, Carl made his stake for being the most important member of the group; if he could scare animals like Negan, he had become invaluable. Carl might still have been a kid, but he proved he has the heart of a lion, albeit a deranged and angry one. In these times, that counts for a lot.

CLASH OF THE TITANS

'End Trails' takes a closer look at the best confrontations between characters. This time, husband and wife team Rick and Lori tear into each other in a domestic unlike any other.

WORDS: **Dan Auty**

WHAT'S THE BEEF?

This confrontation comes soon after the survivors enter the prison. The initial safety that the facility seems to offer is threatened when they learn that the quartet they initially presumed were guards (Dexter, Andrew, Axel and Thomas) are actually inmates. Lori's shocked face says it all – there is a deep concern for the safety of her family. But to Rick they seem like "nice people" who deserve the benefit of the doubt.

ROUND ONE!

Lori has no problem confronting Rick in front of the others in the prison courtyard. It is in moments like this that she speaks to him as the others do – as their leader, making decisions that affect them all – and not as a spouse. She marches right up to him and spells it out – living with "hardened criminals" is not something she feels remotely comfortable with.

ROUND TWO!

Rick deals with Lori's concerns in the way he always did during these early issues. He speaks calmly and reassuringly, pointing out that their group far outnumbers the inmates, and that so far they haven't been a threat.

THE DECIDING BLOW

Reason wins out, and Lori concedes that she might have overreacted. "You're right… I'm a horrible person," she tells him.

AND THE WINNER IS…

On the face of it, Rick wins this particular bout. However, he undermines his victory by throwing out a patronizing quip regarding Lori's pregnancy ("Hormones!").

More crucially, Lori is ultimately proved right, as Thomas turns out to be a psychopathic killer who soon gruesomely beheads Hershel's twin daughters. Should have listened to your wife, Rick! •

THE SECRET DIARY OF A WALKER

It's not easy being a zombie in *The Walking Dead* world, as our week in the life/death of an undead walker shows. Diary entries transcribed by Dan Auty…

MONDAY

Dear Diary…

Jason phoned again. The guy doesn't know when to give up. We dated for a few weeks and he still thinks we should be together. I wouldn't even say *he* was together – his ear dropped off last week and his nose is distinctly loose. He's a nice guy, but does he really think I want to be seen with him looking like that?

TUESDAY

Met up with the girls for lunch. Sophie is on a strict no-brains diet, but the rest of us tucked into a tasty Italian. I think his name was Lucio.

WEDNESDAY

More messages from Jason! Jessica says I should just ignore him, but I'm tempted to go and give him a piece of my mind. There's a lump of it dripping down my forehead – he can have that.

THURSDAY

The girls and I are making plans for a big night out tomorrow – we've not been partying since we got kicked out of Romero's that time. I still say it's not my fault if they employ normos to serve cheap vodka shots. What's a girl to do when she needs a snack halfway through the night?

FRIDAY

We headed up to Alexandria for our night out, but it didn't really go to plan. Jason was there and followed me down the street, moaning about how he still loves me and how he doesn't always smell that bad. Luckily, this other bunch of guys stepped in. Why are all the nice guys either taken or more interested in chopping off heads than sitting down for a nice chat about life after death? Sigh! •

STAYING AL[IVE]

TWDM bets that the majority of people who read *The Walking Dead* comics and/or watch AMC's TV series have their own survival plan come the zombie apocalypse (don't fret, we do too!). But what essential tips could help prevent you from becoming zombie chow? We've scoured the series to find out the best bits of advice that could save your life.

WORDS: Simon Williams

SHUT UP!

As the first living people that Rick encounters after waking from his coma, Morgan Jones and his son Duane were crucial in bringing Rick up to speed on the horrific events of the previous month. But, perhaps more importantly, they also imparted some vital knowledge on how to survive in this new world of the dead – not least, "Shut the eff up!"

Morgan was the first of many characters to stress the importance of keeping quiet, having worked out that the zombies detect their prey by sound, as well as by sight. He also explained that the best (and quietest) way to kill a zombie was to hit them on the head, and notably, during the first visit to the Cynthiana police station, he was quick to stop Rick from wasting ammunition on a zombie that wasn't posing a direct threat.

Later on in the series, science teacher Eugene Porter and soldier Abraham explained how a single gunshot could result in drawing hundreds of zombies to your location, forming a vast herd of the undead.

> ## "WE TRY TO KEEP QUIET… THEY'D COME AFTER US IF THEY KNEW WE WAS HERE."
> MORGAN

IVE

"A GOOD BLOW TO THE HEAD WILL TAKE 'EM OUT." MORGAN

BLUNT OVER BANG

The zombies have had a bum deal when it comes to head traumas since their time on this Earth thanks to those pesky humans. The first demonstration of the effectiveness of a blunt instrument in *The Walking Dead* world was Morgan's resourceful use of a shovel (a weapon probably chosen out of necessity rather than choice).

Morgan may have been the first to be seen adopting such a weapon, but he's by no means been the last. Morgan's shovel is his signature weapon for dispatching zombies, foreshadowing Rick's axe, Tyreese's hammer, and, most prominently, Michonne's katana sword. We'd make a joke about Michonne clearly liking blunt instruments due to her affairs with both Tyreese and Morgan, but that would be far too obvious and probably unfair, especially as two of these characters are no longer with us (at least in the comic – spoiler!).

"THIS HAMMER HAS WORKED JUST FINE FOR ME SO FAR." TYREESE

SENSE & SENSIBILITY

If there's one single character in the series who has proven time and again that he has the skills to survive a zombie apocalypse, it's Glenn. Though not as physically tough as other members of his group, Glenn more than makes up for it with his agility and intelligence. In the early days of the outbreak, it was his bravery and willingness to run into Atlanta for supplies that made him essential to the group's survival.

He unquestionably saved Rick's life at their first meeting in the city, and during the walk back to the Atlanta survivors' camp passed on many pieces of information and advice that would stand Rick in good stead later on: including the zombie infection cycle of 'bite, death, reanimation;' and the importance of always keeping on the move, so the dead can't surround you.

"THOSE THINGS ARE SLOW AS HELL, SO YOU SHOULD BE ABLE TO MANEUVER AROUND THEM."
GLENN

Though he sometimes had a tendency to act rashly, Glenn exhibited a good deal of common sense most of the time. When Rick almost fell while trying to jump between buildings, Glenn wryly pointed out that maybe he should have thrown across his heavy duffel bag first. Soon after, during a supply run back into the city for much-needed weapons and ammunition, he reminded Rick not to grab just anything, pointing out that there's no point carting bullets back to camp if they wouldn't work in the guns they had.

Again his intelligence came into play when he realized that, when looking for gas for the prison generator, it was best to avoid abandoned vehicles and to concentrate on parked cars instead ("I guess nobody would have run out of gas in their parking space now that I think about it...").

"DON'T LET THEM TOUCH YOU. ONE BITE AND IT'S ALL OVER FOR YOU." GLENN

Glenn was never afraid to put himself in danger for the benefit of the wider group, and when it came to practical skills, such as hot-wiring a car or siphoning gas, he showed a remarkable aptitude for survival in a post-apocalyptic world that belied his humble pre-apocalypse life as a pizza delivery boy.

A survivor of the original Atlanta group, Glenn lasted until issue 100, when... Sorry, we can't carry on... We're still in shock, dammit!

BEING HUMAN

One of the longest-surviving members of the original Atlanta group, Andrea's journey from shy law clerk to skilled sharpshooter has been beset by several tragedies that have helped to not only shape her personality, but to give her the skills and toughness to stay alive (and to keep others alive).

Her skills as a long-range sniper have proved pivotal in the defense of both the prison against the Woodbury army and later at the Alexandria Safe-Zone against the Saviors.

While Andrea's proficiency with firearms has allowed her to develop into an effective defense against threats both dead and living, she

"THE MINUTE YOU START THINKING THEY'RE NOT A THREAT… YOU DIE."
ANDREA

has never lost her humanity. Despite having earlier fallen out, it was still Andrea who Allen turned to on his deathbed, asking her to look after his twins after he was gone.

It was only this responsibility that made her consider Dale's proposal to take the RV and leave the prison during a time of crisis. Otherwise, Andrea has always prized loyalty to the group over personal relationships, as was shown in issue 82 when she was quick to punch and then dump Spencer Monroe after he suggested abandoning Alexandria during a zombie attack.

Tasked with taking a group outside the prison for live shooting practice, Andrea was keen to emphasize the importance of staying alert at all times: "Please, and I mean this, do not let your guard down. You live on the other side of those fences long enough, and the danger fades. We're out in the open now, danger is all around us. Don't underestimate the roamers… The minute you start thinking they're not a threat… you die."

BE ALERT, BE VIGILANT, BEWARE

If there's one golden rule in a world where the dead walk, it's this: stay alert. It's no coincidence that the characters who were able to survive for so long in the open were the first to stress the importance of never letting your guard down. It's not just your eyes. Surviving in a world of the dead means utilizing all senses effectively: sight, sounds, and especially smells.

And even if you can't sense the zombies at all, you can be sure they are following you. "That's just how it works out in the open," explained Michonne in issue 27. "We're passing them. Walking right by them without noticing. But *they're* noticing. And following... The longer our trip, the more there will be."

A keen fencer and weightlifter, these pre-apocalypse hobbies have served Michonne well in this new world of the dead. Strong and athletic, it was perhaps no surprise that she was initially drawn to Tyreese, another character defined largely by his abilities; but in contrast to the former NFL pro, Michonne's physical prowess is complemented by a keen intelligence and ability for lateral thinking. Noticing that zombies don't attack each other, she was able

to use her zombified boyfriend, Mike, and his friend as an escort to escape through crowds of roamers (much in the same way that Rick and Glenn covered themselves in zombie body parts to disguise their own smell in Atlanta).

As a coping mechanism, Michonne was often found talking to her dead boyfriend, though she always denied it, sometimes aggressively. But it was a habit she shared with Rick, who revealed to her his own conversations with his dead wife, Lori, on a disconnected telephone.

Despite this eccentricity, Michonne has proven to be extremely resilient both physically and emotionally, particularly after her brutal assault at the hands of The Governor.

Perhaps her biggest failing so far was her decision to convince Tyreese to join her in a counter-attack against Woodbury. Possibly over-estimating their own physical prowess, they soon found themselves outnumbered, leading to Tyreese's capture and horrific execution with Michonne's own sword.

SIZE MATTERS

It's time to get on those exercise bikes and stepmills, folks, because if there's one thing that might give you an edge in the zombie apoc it's being physically fit. Good cardio is key, but it helps if you can put a bit of muscle into the swing of your baseball bat, a la Martinez in season three's 'Arrow On The Doorpost.'

In the comic, the two best examples of prime beef are Tyreese and Abraham, both large and physically imposing men, one an ex-NFL pro football player and the other a former soldier, who survived largely thanks to their size and strength.

Tyreese's muscle and aptitude for up-close melee fighting made him indispensable to the group on a number of occasions, most notably in helping to clear broken-down vehicles soon after joining Rick's group, and then later in clearing the prison of zombies.

Though Abraham was initially distrustful of Rick, he eventually established himself as Rick's right-hand man and

"YOU'RE IN A STATIONARY CAMP AND YOU WERE GOING TO SHOOT ME? NOT VERY SMART." ABRAHAM

the 'muscle' of the group, replacing Tyreese in this role, just as Tyreese had replaced Shane.

But, brute strength was not the only similarity between the two: Tyreese and Abraham also shared a weakness. Both men were prone to bouts of uncontrolled rage that could have ended in disaster. The anger caused by his daughter Julie's death and reanimation caused Tyreese to act with utter recklessness, putting his own life in danger several times. And Abraham confessed to almost murdering Rick after having a gun pointed at him.

Whereas Tyreese's survival lasted so long due to his brute strength, Abraham also benefited from Eugene's knowledge and intelligence: both preferred to be on the move, sharing an aversion to fixed camps, explaining that any noise, especially gunshots, put the group at risk from attack by a herd.

I'M A SCIENTIST, MISTER...

...AND I KNOW *EXACTLY* WHAT CAUSED THIS MESS.

> ## "I HAVE TWO THINGS GOING FOR ME. I AM EXTREMELY INTELLIGENT. AND I AM A GOOD LIAR."
> ### EUGENE

met Rick's group at Hershel's home, he was able to persuade Rick to leave the farm and join them on their journey to Washington DC by cautioning them on their use of firearms and the risks associated with maintaining a stationary camp. It's also Eugene who first explained the concept of a zombie herd.

"There's a radius around this place," he explained. "A limit to how far this sound will travel. Picture that area as a net, and every time you make a sound as loud as a gunshot, you catch every dead person in that net, and you drive them here. Eventually you will be overcome if you use firearms so carelessly."

In the TV series, Milton (played by Dallas Roberts) seems to have taken on many of the characteristics of Eugene. Although weak (both physically and willed), Milton has stayed alive so long by using his smarts to impress someone much stronger, The Governor, to look after him. But, as soon as Milton's usefulness came to an end, Philip Blake simply ate him up and spat him out – making him do what he least wanted, take a human life.

MMM... BRAINS!

Of all the characters in *The Walking Dead*, Eugene Porter employed perhaps the most unique survival strategy. The former high school science teacher believed he didn't have what it took (physically) to stay alive, and that he was better off attaching himself to someone who did.

Using his knowledge and a couple of tricks – such as making a simple compass from a magnetized needle, and pretending to maintain contact with his superiors on an old battery-operated radio – he was able to convince Abraham that he was a top government scientist with classified information about the origin of the zombie plague. At the same time, he styled his hair in a mullet, knowing it would disguise his intelligence.

In a way, he was no different to Rosita, only Rosita was able to use her looks to gain Abraham's protection.

Despite his charade, it's clear that Eugene is indeed a clever individual. When he, Abraham and Rosita first

HU-UNGH!

WROKK!

"EVENTUALLY YOU WILL BE OVERCOME IF YOU USE FIREARMS SO CARELESSLY."
EUGENE

I HAVE TWO THINGS GOING FOR ME.

I AM EXTREMELY INTELLIGENT.

AND I AM A GOOD LIAR.

I DIDN'T HAVE A LOT OF OPTIONS.

SURVIVAL GAME

A *TWDM* SPECIAL QUIZ

1.

YOU'VE BEEN AT HOME LISTENING TO REPORTS OF WALKER ATTACKS AND LOOTING ON THE TV FOR THE PAST FEW HOURS. ALL OF A SUDDEN THERE'S A GROANING NOISE FROM OUTSIDE, AND YOU HEAR SOMEONE (OR SOMETHING) THUDDING AGAINST YOUR FRONT DOOR. THE FIRST THING YOU GRAB IS…

A) The closest heavy object to hand. A plumber's wrench. You can smash this walker's head in and then finish fixing the faucet later.

B) You don't need to grab anything, you're already carrying. One shot at head height through the door should do the job – living or dead, makes no difference to you.

C) The TV remote. Thumb the mute button. If you keep quiet maybe they'll go away…

D) Your journal. This is history happening right here and now. The world will want to know what you were thinking.

It's been a pretty heavy and emotional book so far, so how about a bit of fun?
TWDM has put together this little quiz for you – don't worry, there's no math involved (unless you include counting up your answers, so scratch that, actually there is some math involved). Ever wondered what type of survivor you'd be if (or even when) the zombie apocalypse comes? Are you the kind to help a fellow survivor, or more of a lone wolf? Find out here…
QUIZMASTER: Simon Williams

2.

YOU ENCOUNTER A GROUP OF OTHER SURVIVORS AT A CAMPSITE JUST OUTSIDE THE CITY. HOW DO YOU MAKE YOURSELF USEFUL SO THEY'LL LET YOU JOIN?

A) Well, for a start, you need to have a word with whoever's in charge around here about why there isn't even a lookout. One person with a rifle on that RV would have a perfect view of the surrounding area.
B) Who says you want to join? But safety in numbers and all that. You're happy to go and collect firewood alone, get some peace and quiet until you can decide whether it's best for you to stick around.
C) You've still got your backpack full of stuff from your last sneak trip into the nearby city. Toilet paper and chocolate anyone?
D) You'll think of something. It's clear that this ragtag bunch of losers needs a real leader. Don't think they're quite ready for you yet, so you're best biding your time until you can make a move.

3.

YOU'RE HEADING DEEP INTO THE CITY TO SCAVENGE ESSENTIAL SUPPLIES FOR YOUR GROUP. THE FIRST THING YOU PACK IS…

A) A hammer. If you're not caving in walkers' brains, you can use it to break into stores. And a hammer never needs reloading.
B) An extra bag, for all the goodies you're gonna put aside for yourself. No reason the rest of the group needs to know about it.
C) Baseball cap. It'll keep the sun out of your eyes and you prefer to travel light anyway. Weapons only attract walkers.
D) You'd be more use staying put, someone's got to keep an eye on things around here. Why is it always you anyway? How about someone else goes this time?

4.

YOUR GROUP HAS BEEN ALLOWED TO SETTLE ON A NEARBY FARM AND EVERYTHING'S GOING SWELL. BUT IT'S NOT LONG UNTIL YOU FIND OUT ABOUT YOUR HOST'S OTHER 'GUESTS,' THE ONES HE KEEPS LOCKED UP IN THE BIG BARN. HOW DO YOU REACT?

A) Tell him he's wrong for keeping walkers on his property and that you'll take care of it – you can't have your group put at risk like that, it just has to be done.

B) You're not putting your life at risk one moment longer. Who cares what the old man thinks? Get a small team together and bust those barn doors wide open and make light work of whatever comes out. If your host has a problem with that then maybe you should take his farm off him.

C) You try and reason with your host. Explain why keeping walkers that close to where you all sleep is definitely a bad idea. But for now they're not bothering anyone in there. You need to tread carefully. You don't want to risk upsetting your host, he may get angry and throw you and your group out.

D) You have to wonder why a man would keep a barn full of walkers, and what he does with them when no one's looking. Maybe you've got more in common with him than you thought.

5.

AFTER AN ENCOUNTER WITH WALKERS, A GUY IN THE GROUP GETS BITTEN ON THE HAND AND WILL EVENTUALLY TURN. TO PUT HIM OUT OF HIS MISERY, WOULD YOU…?

A) Wait for him to turn and then put a bullet in his brain. Only way to be sure. Shame you weren't there when he got bitten, your machete would have taken that arm off at the elbow in one go. Maybe stopped the infection before it took.

B) Shoot him right there and then. Why wait for him to turn? Who cares what the guy's wife thinks? She'll thank you later. After she's stopped sobbing and cleaned her husband's brains off her face.

C) Make his last moments as comfortable as possible, even if it means using the last of the morphine to make sure he doesn't feel a thing. You'd want them to do the same for you. Then a bullet.

D) Put the guy back to work – after all it's only a flesh wound, and he can still be useful until he turns. Actually, now you think about it, he can be useful after he turns, too. Maybe provide some entertainment for the rest of the group.

6.

YOUR GROUP FINDS AN ABANDONED PRISON IN THE MIDDLE OF NOWHERE. IT WOULD MAKE A PERFECT BASE. ONLY TROUBLE IS, IT'S NOT QUITE ABANDONED – IT'S OVERRUN WITH WALKERS. BUT IT'S TOO GOOD AN OPPORTUNITY TO PASS UP. YOU PLAN TO…

A) Pick off as many walkers as you can with your rifle. Then shotguns and blunt weapons for the close-up work. You'll have that place cleared out in no time at all.
B) Get in there first and pick the best cell for yourself, away from everyone else.
C) Attract the zombies to the fence and shove a blade through the gaps in the wire – straight between the eyes – and take them out that way. It's stupid to rush in with all guns blazing. This way there's always a fence between you and danger.
D) Let some other guys take the risk. Wait for them to clean the place up, then turn up afterwards and take it off them.

> LITTLE PIG, LITTLE PIG.
> LET ME IN.

7.

A STRANGER TURNS UP AT THE GATE AND STARTS SHOUTING HIS MOUTH OFF, DEMANDING THAT YOU LET HIM AND ALL HIS FRIENDS IN OR YOU'LL BE SORRY. DO YOU…?

A) Take him out with one shot (you already saw him coming a mile off from your vantage point in the church tower). Then put a few rounds into that bus wreck down the road, where his friends are hiding. They'll scatter like rats… if they've got any sense.

B) Let him in. He seems like a stronger character than the idiots you've got in charge at the moment. And if it turns out you're wrong, you'll kill him yourself.
C) Keep the gate closed. You don't need any trouble, as long as you're in here and they're out there.
D) Open the gate and welcome this guy and his friends in. Make them feel at home. Give them some coffee and cake. Make them feel like they've nothing to fear. And then, when they least expect it… Don't forget to save the heads!

8.

WHEN GOING IN TO CLEAR AN AREA OF WALKERS, WHAT'S YOUR WEAPON OF CHOICE?

A) A hammer – you like to keep things up close and personal.

B) A samurai sword – a couple of quick swishes and you can put your feet up and have a nice cup of tea.

C) Someone else. In other words, let the big muscular men sort it out for you.

D) A tank. OK, you don't know how to fire the thing, but you like the pleasant squishing sound it makes as it runs over entrails and such.

9.

YOU DISCOVER A GROUP OF CANNIBALS AND THEY'VE EATEN ONE OF YOUR FELLOW SURVIVORS. YOU OVERPOWER THEM, BUT THEN HOW DO YOU HANDLE THE SITUATION?

A) Execution. There's no coming back from that, it's the best thing for them. Besides, if you leave them alive they may try to eat some other unwary traveler.

B) Shout "What the fuck?" a lot and then mow them down in a hail of bullets.

C) Throw up. The very idea revolts you. But you're a humanitarian and you can't kill them, despite how disgusting you think they are.

D) Ask if there are any leftovers. You're starving. Om-nom-nom!

AND YOU ARE...

MOSTLY As:
You fancy yourself as the hero type, like **Rick** or **Andrea**, not afraid to make the difficult decisions – after all, someone has to. And you don't mind getting up close and personal with walkers, like **Tyreese** or **Abraham**. Nothing like an intense session of

zombie bashing to get the blood pumping.

MOSTLY Bs:
You're more of a lone wolf, like **Merle** – always looking out for number one. It's the only way to survive in this world of the walking dead. Besides, who needs other survivors? They'll only slow you down, right?

MOSTLY Cs:
Like **Glenn**, you're a team player, but you believe in caution over confrontation. And like **Lori** or **Hershel**, you're not afraid to put Rick and the

others to rights when needed. Of course, sometimes there's just no avoiding the dead, and if you have to take one out then it's best to keep things nice and quiet, just in case Mr Walker has a few hundred of his friends in the neighborhood.

MOSTLY Ds:

You're a true survivor, but you're a cruel, depraved despot in the making. You're not afraid to get your hands dirty every now and again, but you're happiest when others do the dirty work for you. You may still be human but you lost your humanity a long time ago. What's your name again? Or do you prefer **The Governor**? •

10.

YOU'VE MADE FRIENDS WITH ANOTHER COMMUNITY OF SURVIVORS NEARBY, AND THEY'VE ASKED TO TRADE RESOURCES. AS LEADER OF YOUR GROUP, WHAT WILL YOU OFFER THEM IN TRADE FOR FOOD?

A) Muscle. You know how to handle yourself and you can keep the two communities free from walker hordes.

B) Why trade? You don't need any of their lousy food anyway, you've still got some army rations left, and this unmarked can of something...

C) Whatever they need. You're open to setting up a really strong trade relationship with these guys. They seem nice.

D) Oh, you've got food, have you? Gimme! Gimme! Gimme!

DEARLY BELOVED....

From the very start, *The Walking Dead* has strived to create a world where no one is safe and any character can die (with perhaps the exception of Rick). What follows over the next few pages is a roll call of the dearly (and occasionally, not so dearly) departed. Who's dead? Who's undead? It's a list with a lot of red ink. For the sake of brevity, *TWDM* has chosen the most important, the most gruesome and the most horrific deaths in the saga.

WORDS: Stuart Barr

NICE GIRLS ARE FINISHED FIRST

One of the first high-profile casualties in the comic series was Amy, sister of Andrea. Bitten by a walker when trying to take a toilet break, Amy is then shot by her sister before she can reanimate. This death was an early sign that being a nice person is no protection from Robert Kirkman's red ink pen.

LORI CRASH

The next major casualty in the comic book was Rick Grimes's former police partner, Shane. Believing Rick dead, Shane has fallen in love with his wife, Lori. So following Rick's return and stewing with jealousy, Shane suffered something of a meltdown, pulling a gun on him, only to be shot dead by Rick and Lori's son, Carl. Shot by a kid – not something you want etched on your tombstone!

Later, when Rick realizes that you don't need to be bitten to return, he treks back to Shane's grave, digs him up, and shoots him again, leaving his body lying in the freshly exhumed grave with a terse, "I'm not burying you again, you son of a bitch."

"I COULDN'T SLEEP, KNOWING YOU WERE DOWN THERE. WOULD YOU HAVE LEFT ME? YOU WERE A GOOD MAN, SHANE. I DON'T KNOW WHY YOU DID WHAT YOU DID... BUT YOU WERE A GOOD MAN."

RICK TO SHANE'S REANIMATED CORPSE

LOVED TO DEATH

One of the saddest deaths from the Atlanta group was Carol (Sophia's mother). Going off the psychological deep end after lover Tyreese has an affair, she gradually becomes suicidal, finally offering herself up to a zombie who rips into her throat.

Dying she says, "Oh good, you do like me," like a Sally Field Oscar speech in Hell.

"I DON'T REALLY HAVE ANYONE TO TALK TO. SO I FIGURED I'D INTRODUCE MYSELF. I'M CAROL."
CAROL MEETS HER FATE

"DON'T WORRY, HE'S GOING TO COME BACK. I DIDN'T HURT HIS BRAINS." BEN, AFTER KILLING HIS BROTHER

THE SORRY SAGA OF ALLEN, DONNA, BEN AND BILLY

The Walking Dead has seen entire bloodlines rubbed out. Witness the tragedy of Allen, Donna and their sons, Ben and Billy. Part of the original Atlanta group, Donna died during the unfortunate stopover at the Wiltshire Estates, killed and consumed by zombies. Husband Allen goes next, bitten during a zombie hunt in the prison. He dies in his sleep and is shot by Rick.

Dale and Andrea then adopt the couple's sons. The adults fail to notice that a traumatized Ben is becoming a psychopath. On the road to DC, Ben kills and mutilates his brother, Billy. While the grown-ups dither, Carl kills Ben in the night.

JOCK STRAPPED

Tyreese, a former NFL player, joins the group post-Atlanta. When the prison is threatened by the nearby community, Woodbury, headed by their charismatic and villainous leader The Governor, he and Michonne make an ill-judged attempt to mount an offense. The play fails to go off as smoothly as on a football pitch.

He is captured and used as leverage in an attempt to access the prison. Knowing there is nothing he can do to save him, Rick refuses to comply, so The Governor beheads Tyreese with Michonne's stolen katana. In a coda, his severed head reanimates, only to be finally put to rest by Michonne.

HUNGER PAINS

There are few exits from *The Walking Dead* as hardcore as that of Dale. After the group reconstitute following the prison massacre, they run into a group of cannibals stalking human prey for meat. The one-legged Dale is captured and awakes to find he is being gradually butchered, one limb at a time. What the hunters don't know is that Dale has been bitten and is already dying. Dale takes grim satisfaction from the knowledge that his leg is poisoning his captors.

After his friends find and brutally kill the hunters, he succumbs to his wounds, dying in the arms of his lover, Andrea, who must shoot him post-mortem. That's romance in *The Walking Dead* universe for you, ladies and gents.

"I'M TAINTED MEAT! YOU'RE EATING TAINTED MEAT! TAINTED MEAT! HA! HA! HA! HA!"
DALE LAUGHS IN THE FACE OF DEATH

MORGAN'S FREE, MAN

Way back in issue one, the first survivors encountered by Rick following his escape from the hospital were Morgan Jones and his son, Duane. They remained in the small town of Cynthiana at the end of the issue. However, Rick always hoped to see them again. So, when on the road to Washington DC the group pass nearby the town, he sets out using the excuse of emptying his police station full of weapons and supplies.

This is one of Rick's most disastrous leadership decisions. He discovers Morgan alive, but Duane zombified. The experience of living with his dead son, knowing he had failed to protect him, has driven Morgan to the shadowy outskirts of a town called Sanity. Nevertheless, Rick cannot leave him and opts to take him back to the group. On the return journey, they run into a vast zombie herd, total their vehicle, lose the supplies, and have to flee with thousands of zombies in pursuit. Morgan survives and gradually recovers, but in the chaos of the Alexandria Safe-Zone perimeter wall collapsing, he is bitten. Michonne severs the affected limb, but to no avail, so she must remove his head too.

SERGEANT-AT-ARMS

Ex-army sergeant Abraham Ford joined the group shortly after the events at the prison. He may have been one of *The Walking Dead*'s toughest characters, but that didn't stop him from dying outside of the Alexandria Safe-Zone without even hearing the crossbow arrow that killed him.

No blaze of glory; just there one minute, gone the next.

"LUCILLE IS A VAMPIRE BAT. WHAT? WAS THE JOKE THAT BAD?"
NEGAN, AFTER BASHING IN GLENN'S BRAINS

STRIKE ONE!

Most recently, in the most Earth-shattering murder since Lori and Judith, much-loved character Glenn met a grisly end. A staple of the comic since issue two, Glenn is accompanying Rick on another crusade, this one against bandits who are raiding the survivor communities around Washington. Grossly underestimating the marauders' size and strength, they are ambushed by their leader, Negan, who plays a horrible game of tic-tac-toe with the captives before smashing Glenn's head in with a baseball bat (nicknamed Lucille) like an overstuffed piñata.

THE NIGHT OF THE LONG KNIVES

Issue 48, in which The Governor lays siege upon the prison, is an absolute bloodbath – Robert Kirkman has never been more ruthless! In a single issue, seven principal characters and a horde of Woodbury militia are wiped out. The prison is so overrun with zombies that while the ultimate fate of many of these victims is never shown, it is clear they are now zombie chow.

As the pages ran red, victims included:

Alice – The Doctor's assistant who helped Rick and Glenn escape from Woodbury becomes another Governor victim.

Axel – The biker prisoner is shot early on in the skirmish with The Governor's men.

Billy Greene – Last surviving son of Hershel Greene, fatally shot in front of his father.

Hershel – Seeing his son killed destroys his will to live. He passively accepts a bullet from The Governor. Last words: "Dear God... Please. Just kill me."

Patricia – A survivor from Hershel's farm, also shot.

Philip Blake – The Governor himself, shot by Lilly Caul, one of his own militia members.

Lori and Judith – In one of the most shocking and unexpected panels of art in the whole of *The Walking Dead* (in fact, we'd go as far as to say in any comic in the last 10 years – yes, more shocking than Captain America being assassinated), Lori is shot by Lilly with her newborn baby, Judith, either killed by the same bullet or crushed under Lori's body. Lilly's horror at killing an unarmed mother and child motivates her to kill The Governor. •

THE TV DEPARTED

While the AMC televisual adaptation of the comic book has taken plot strands and characters from the comics, it has also developed in its own direction. As such, it cannot be taken for granted that characters will live or die in the same fashion as they do in the comic.

The roll call of the TV dead includes...

Amy – Her demise as the Atlanta camp is overrun is almost identical to the comic.

Sophia – Practically the entire plot of season two consists of the hunt for the missing daughter of Carol, until she is eventually discovered zombified in Hershel's barn. Sophia is still alive in the comic book, but Carol, dead in the comics, is still breathing in the TV show.

Dale – The liberal conscience of the TV show, Dale is attacked and mortally wounded by a lone walker. Rick cannot bring himself to shoot Dale. Instead, Daryl takes his gun and performs the deed.

Shane – The TV series keeps tensions burning between Rick, Shane and Lori far longer than in the comic. At the end of season two ('Better Angels'), Shane gets Rick alone under a pretense. Realizing Shane means to kill him, he waits for him to make a move, then kills him with his knife. Unbeknown to Rick, Carl has followed them and when Shane reanimates, Carl shoots him.

T-Dog – Becomes zombie chow in season three's 'Killer Within,' saving Carol from walkers.

Lori – A heart-breaking moment as Lori dies during childbirth. And then it's up to her son, Carl, to make sure she doesn't return as one of the undead...

TOP 5

We pick five of our *Walking Dead* favorites, from characters and moments to lines of dialogue, weapons, deaths and more.
WORDS: Louisa Owen

WOMEN ON THE FRONTLINE
Five moments of Female Fortitude

SHIT.

I REALLY DIDN'T THINK IT'D BE THIS BAD. WE WERE GONE FOR **FIVE DAYS.**

5. THE FUTURE LOOKS ROSIE!

Building a new society requires hard work from everyone involved, but one character that really seems to have stepped up to the plate recently is Rosita. Leading out the herders for a five-day mission and then coming back straight into building work is probably not what we would have imagined for Abraham's jilted lover. She wass always a strong character for sure, but before the time jump, she was more of a background beauty. She truly adapted into a leader, a woman at the helm of getting things done.

◇◇◇◇◇◇◇◇◇◇◇◇◇◇◇◇◇◇◇◇◇◇◇◇◇

4. HOW TO MAKE A KILLER ENTRANCE!

Michonne is certainly one of the strongest female characters in the comic, but even after all she's achieved, her entrance is still one of her most impressive moments. It's not only because of the sheer awesomeness of her taking out a bunch of walkers with ease, while Otis cowers in the background, it's also to do with what she'd achieved before we meet her. Could any other character have stayed alive and sane (for the most part) being alone for so long? In the words of Rick, "That woman's got to be as tough as nails."

THROK!

3. DOCTOR'S ORDERS!

In a zombie apocalypse, medical knowledge is indispensable to survival. It's actually amazing that there have been no maniacal medics, bartering their wares for power… maybe there really is something to the Hippocratic Oath! None of the doctors of *The Walking Dead* appear to last that long, but one of the most important physicians was Denise Cloyd of Alexandria. She really proved she was a doctor above all else when, regardless of the fact she had been bitten and would surely die if her arm was not amputated, she chose to spend her last hours saving the lives of Heath and Carl. She could have lived, but she chose not to for the good of others.

2. GUNNING FOR THE ENEMY!

Everyone would like to think that come the breakdown of civilized society, they could step up and be the gun-toting tough guy. The truth is, few could; Rick is the obvious example, but possibly the best from the comic is its most talented sharpshooter – Andrea. Back in issue 113, it seemed Negan's lackey Connor had bested Rick's right-hand woman, as a body was seen falling from the watchtower after their vicious fight. But, if the chips are down, we would place our bet on Andrea any day of the week. It's going to take more than a knife-wielding maniac to take out Andrea – she doesn't die (at least in the comics).

1. LABOR PAINS!

Childbirth is always described as one of the most painful experiences a woman can go through, but transport that process to a soon-to-be-besieged prison, with a doctor who never really trained and whose answer to "I hope you're ready!" is "Oh, crap!" – well, it's enough to cause even the hardiest soul some worry. Lori dealt with the whole pregnancy unbelievably well – never overly dramatic – and it's how she deals with the birth, too, that makes her top of our list. She just gets on with it. It's a different kind of strength than that shown by Andrea or Michonne, but it's invaluable in a world where at some point society will need to rebuild.

CHOICE CUTS

In each 'Choice Cuts,' we examine one of *The Walking Dead*'s most memorable characters, picking out their brightest moments, their darkest hours and, well, their choicest cuts. In this feature, our beady eye focuses on the katana-wielding Michonne.

WORDS: Dan Auty

MICHONNE

DEAD VOICES

One of the first indicators that there was more to Michonne than just attitude and sword skills came soon after her arrival. Andrea found her sitting alone, talking at length to something or someone. Michonne denied she was doing any such thing – until much later on, when she confessed to Rick that these were conversations with her long-dead boyfriend, Mike. She explained that she imagines he is in control of her situation, telling her what to do: "It makes things easier. Easier to deal with."

HER DARKEST HOUR

Michonne has been through a lot, but her ordeal at the hands of The Governor stands as one of the most shocking ever inflicted on any major character in the entire series. Imprisoned in Woodbury, Michonne was bound, beaten and raped over a period of several days by the town's cruel ruler.

But Michonne proved to be stronger than any of The Governor's previous victims; when Rick rescued her, instead of fleeing, she sought out her tormentor and unleashed hell.

"I'M NOT CRYING FOR ME. I'M CRYING FOR YOU. I THINK ABOUT ALL THE THINGS I'M GOING TO DO TO YOU AND IT MAKES ME CRY. IT SCARES ME."
Michonne hooks The Governor

HER GREATEST MOMENT

The Walking Dead is filled with many thrilling, splatter happy scenes of Michonne slicing her way through hordes of zombies. However, her true moment of personal achievement came not in the midst of a bloodbath, but when she finally hung up her blade upon arrival in the Alexandria Safe Zone.

Recalling the months of slaughter that she had inflicted on both the living and the dead (including her turned boyfriend and his best friend attacking her), she placed her katana on the wall of her new home with the simple words, "I'm through with you." For a few pages at least, it almost seemed possible that life really could start again.

KATANA-RAMA

Let's face it, personal growth and heartfelt emotion are all very well, but that wasn't the reason Michonne was voted number 86 on *IGN*'s Top 100 Comic Book Heroes list. She is super bad-ass, a fearless warrior with a sword and, while a gun might be a more effective weapon, nothing looks better on the page than a blade chopping through a walker's neck.

The most exciting scene of Michonne mayhem came during her time in Woodbury, when she was forced to fight in one of The Governor's crowd-pleasing gladiatorial bouts. Reunited with her trusty katana, Michonne disobeyed orders and, after quickly decapitating her opponent, dispatched the half-dozen walkers surrounding her. It was such an aggressive display, it almost turned The Governor's people against him.

She may have been thrown back into a cell, but it was a key moment that let readers know that you must *never* count Michonne out.

"STAY CLOSE TO ME!"
Michonne's first words

LOVE LIKE BLOOD, PART 1

Starting relationships and enjoying romance isn't exactly easy in a bleak post-apocalyptic world, but even so, Michonne has had less luck than most. When she first met Rick's group, she had her jawless, armless, decaying boyfriend and his best friend chained up on a leash to "mostly" keep the other zombies from attacking her. Told she cannot join the group with them in tow, she hacked off their heads without a moment's hesitation.

Sentiment is not one of her weak spots.

"I'M SORRY I'M SUCH A BITCH. I DON'T MEAN TO BE, IT'S JUST… IT'S THE WAY I AM."
Michonne apologizes to Morgan

LOVE LIKE BLOOD, PART 2

Michonne began a passionate affair with ex-NFL star Tyreese, right under the nose of his current lady Carol. Their relationship continued on and off, and was strengthened by their attempts to defend the prison from The Governor's forces. Unfortunately, things came to an unpleasant end courtesy of Michonne's nemesis. And if that wasn't bad enough, Tyreese's cranium made an unexpected reappearance a few issues later, forcing Michonne into making another difficult choice.

LOVE LIKE BLOOD, PART 3

Michonne's last beau was Morgan. Although she treated Morgan in her usual *friendly* way – a mix of disdain and pity – it is clear that these two had a bond stronger than any of her previous relationships. Alas, the course of true love never seems to run very smoothly in Robert Kirkman's dark, zombie-infested world, and Michonne lost another lover to the undead infection. In one of Michonne's most powerful scenes, she confessed her true feelings to Morgan as he succumbed to the virus, before unsheathing her sword once more.

CHARLIE ADLARD'S FAVORITE MICHONNE MOMENT

"After the prison saga when they're all dispersed, the first time Rick and Carl encounter Michonne again. Carl is being threatened by a zombie in a car – it's trying to get in at him through the window and Michonne shoves her sword right through the back of its head and out its mouth. That's still one of my favorite shots of Michonne. I think I really captured her character in that."

ROBERT KIRKMAN'S FAVORITE MICHONNE MOMENT

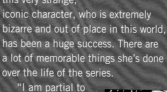

"Picking a single moment as a favorite is very difficult. Michonne is a fan favorite for a reason. Throwing her into the mix, this very strange, iconic character, who is extremely bizarre and out of place in this world, has been a huge success. There are a lot of memorable things she's done over the life of the series.

"I am partial to the scene in issue 49 where she stabs Tyreese's severed head though. It's a moment I feel defines her as a character and says a lot about *The Walking Dead* world. She loved this man. And she can only afford him a single tear, before moving on. She's tough as nails. That's why people love her." •

MAGGIE

Given the role of women in *The Walking Dead*, it seemed only right that we focus on one of both the comic and TV series' most enduring female characters for our Choice Cuts: Maggie Greene. She's been part of the comic for more than 120 issues and on the show since season two: she's come a long way from being a disinterested farm girl to an assured survivor and, in the comics, the inspiring leader of the Hilltop. Here are some of our favorite Maggie moments.

WORDS: Louisa Owen

FIRST APPEARANCE

It was way back in issue 10 that Maggie Greene first came on the scene; introduced by her father Hershel as, "the one holding that chair down," she could not have looked less interested in meeting Rick and the gang. There was nothing in that Greene introductory page to suggest it would be Maggie who would become one of the most central characters in the comic, or that she even wanted to be.

Despite her initial reluctance, however, it didn't take long for something (or someone) to catch her eye, and that was Glenn. Noticing his attraction to Carol, Maggie and her future husband-to-be had a frank discussion about relationships that left one thing clear about Hershel's daughter: she's definitely not shy.

DESPITE BEING SURROUNDED BY THE LIVING DEAD, GLENN AND MAGGIE DO MANAGE TO ENJOY SOME OF THE 'NORMALITIES' OF MARRIED LIFE.

WHEN THE GOING GETS TOUGH

After watching many of her siblings die in the barn, the brutal murder of her younger sisters, Susie and Rachel, seemed to push Maggie over the edge. She told Glenn she couldn't love him anymore, as he too would probably die. It seemed like everything was about to fall apart for Maggie, but then came a major turning point.

When her twin sisters' murderer is identified as former prison inmate Thomas Richards, Tyreese threatens to kill him unless he stops, but Maggie, well, she's not so restrained. She shoots Thomas in the back and head six times. She doesn't bat an eyelid as she stares down at her handiwork.

This girl just out bad-assed Tyreese!

FOR BETTER OR FOR WORSE

Despite being surrounded by the living dead, Glenn and Maggie do manage to enjoy some of the 'normalities' of married life: the difficulties of sex after the apocalypse; the stresses of a nine-to-five where a bad day at the office ends in undeath; and even, in the more refreshingly mundane moments of *The Walking Dead*, watching your partner be 'that guy' at a party...

When the residents of the Alexandria Safe-Zone throw a party for Rick and the rest of the new arrivals, Glenn has a smidgeon too much to drink and, well, we've all been there. It ends with an amused Rick escorting him off the premises. Maggie is very much the sensible wife, trying to take care of him, eyes closed in embarrassment as he slurs through conversation, and the one who stays up waiting for the kids to come home.

MAGGIE SETS A FINE MATERNAL EXAMPLE, AND SOPHIA SOON INHERITS SOME OF THAT GREENE FIRE.

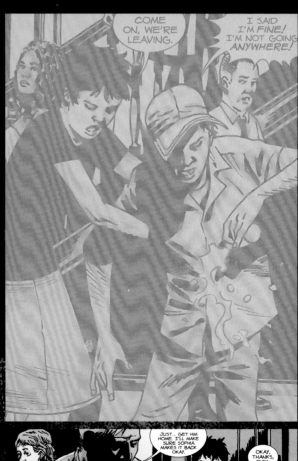

ROMANTIC DALLIANCE

The only real hint we get of Maggie's pre-apocalyptic romantic entanglements is that she had a boyfriend she didn't much care for. Her famous first pass at Glenn didn't exactly reek of romance either. However, it very quickly became clear how important her relationship with Glenn was to her. After the tragic events in the barn, Glenn spends the night in her room. Hershel nearly had a heart attack when he discovered them, but Maggie stands up for herself and isn't afraid to admit that she already loves Glenn.

HER DARKEST HOUR

There have been a few dark times for Maggie, so it's quite difficult to pick just one. But a real low point came in issue 51, when, unable to cope with what had happened to her family, she decided to hang herself. It was a tense moment for readers, made that much tenser by Abraham waving a gun around, determined to shoot her before she reanimated.

Luckily, Maggie survived the ordeal, but it raised huge questions about how she would cope with all the death that surrounds our survivors every day. In the end, her resolve to be there for her husband and adopted daughter is what pushed her back into fighting for life. Even when the brutal death of her husband came, she was strong enough to think about Sophia and her unborn child, and chose to keep going.

GRIT AND DETERMINATION

Lauren Cohan has certainly won fans over with her fiery, kick-ass portrayal of Maggie, but towards the end of season four, it wasn't so much her fantastic fighting but her sheer, unflinching determination to find Glenn that impressed. Regardless of whether it was in a bus full of walkers or in the unknown quantity that was Terminus, she was going to find him. She even writes messages to the man in walker blood, for crying out loud.

When she believes Bob and Sasha will slow down her mission to find her love, she leaves them behind (albeit temporarily). Maggie was a woman on a mission. What made her hunt even more effective was the fact it was matched exactly by Glenn's determination to find her.

MAGGIE FACT FILE

NAME: Maggie Greene
PLAYED IN TV SERIES BY: Lauren Cohan
CURRENT AGE: 23
JOB: Student, farm girl (pre-apocalypse); Leader of the Hilltop (post-apocalypse)
RELATIONSHIPS POST-APOCALYPSE: Glenn (husband), Sophia (adopted daughter), Hershel Greene (son); the Greene family (all dead) – Hershel (father), Billy (brother), Rachel (sister), Susie (sister), Lacey (sister), Arnold (brother), Shawn (brother)
LIKES: Glenn, Hershel (dad), Hershel (son), Sophia (adopted daughter), Greene family, Hilltop, Rick and Carl Grimes
DISLIKES: Negan, death, college
FIRST APPEARANCE: Issue #10
CURRENT STATUS: Alive (in both TV show and comic book).

BECOMING A MOM

Maggie was tried and tested as a maternal figure early on in the comic. In the wake of Carol's death, Sophia attached herself very strongly to Maggie. While it may have been worrying how quickly and vehemently she claimed Maggie as her true mother, Maggie took it upon herself to play that role. After a shaky start involving a tree and

some rope, she adapted remarkably well, always putting Sophia first, and telling Glenn that her priority was just to find a safe place for her adopted daughter to grow up.

Maggie sets a fine maternal example, and Sophia soon inherits some of that Greene fire, beating up a couple of bullies in the Hilltop who go after her friend. Like mother, like daughter.

HER FINEST MOMENT

It's a long way from being that disinterested girl at the Greene farmhouse to becoming the leader of the Hilltop community, but there is no question as to Maggie's qualifications for the job. When the people of the Hilltop don't want to join Rick in the fight against Negan, Maggie delivers a rousing speech that puts then-leader Gregory truly in his place. She makes it abundantly clear what and whom they should be fighting for, even giving the spineless Gregory a punch for good measure. How can you say no to a woman as passionate as that?

WHEN THE PEOPLE OF HILLTOP DON'T WANT TO JOIN RICK IN THE FIGHT AGAINST NEGAN, MAGGIE DELIVERS A ROUSING SPEECH THAT PUTS THEN-LEADER GREGORY TRULY IN HIS PLACE.

HOW THE HILL WAS WON

If you really have to make a speech, make it a good one:

"You are not stupid people. Don't allow your leader to ruin your lives. Is anyone here happy with the status quo? You like working so hard to give Negan and his people half?... Rick thinks if we band together this guy is done for. We can't let him down now. He's trying to help us all! If Rick Grimes says this is something we need to do, something that can be done... He's someone we can trust. If there's one thing that I'm certain of... I know this... I believe in Rick Grimes."

TILL DEATH DO US PART

KEEPING ROMANCE ALIVE IN AN UNDEAD WORLD

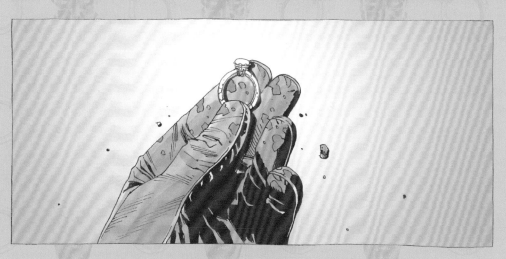

All you need is love, according to the song, but lasting relationships can't survive on love alone. Respect, support, communication, and mutual attraction are just some of the important ingredients necessary to keep a romantic partnership alive. Not being bitten by a hungry walker would be another vital relationship tip for those living in *The Walking Dead* world. *TWDM* looks at how the survivors of the apocalypse prevent death and reanimation spoiling a good marriage. **WORDS:** Stuart Barr

Any first year psychology student will be familiar with the theory of Maslow's Hierarchy of Needs, which ranks the physiological and emotional requirements for psychological well-being. Physiological needs (food, shelter, clothing) must be met first, to ensure simple survival. Then, the needs necessary for safety (shelter, health, security) must be fulfilled. After these basic and very functional needs have been satisfied, emotional needs can be addressed. The first of these is the need for love and belonging. All well and good, but that's not so easy to do when you have hordes of flesh-hungry undead constantly on your tail.

So how does *The Walking Dead* present human intimacy? In a post-zombie apocalypse world, do the flowers of romance still smell sweet? These are some of the most profound, and the most disturbing, relationships in the post-zombie apocalypse world.

TO HAVE AND TO HOLD

Rick and Lori Grimes' relationship was built on mutual respect. This was a healthy marriage. They were compatible physically and psychologically, and just as mentally strong as each other. Lori regularly challenged her husband's decisions and actions in ways that were predominantly constructive, although some fans (presumably all male) interpreted this as 'nagging,' making her not the most beloved of characters in the series.

> ## "RICK AND I ARE THE MOST COMPATIBLE PEOPLE ON EARTH. WE ARE PERFECT FOR EACH OTHER."
> ## LORI ABOUT RICK

The strength of the relationship was first tested when it emerged that Lori had had a sexual encounter with Rick's best friend, Shane. This took place on the way to Atlanta when she was unsure whether Rick was alive or not. It was a moment of physical need during a dark period, and no more. Lori dismissed it as a 'fling' and, when Rick returned to her, Shane was unceremoniously rejected. When Rick discovered the truth, he was able to quickly compartmentalize and forgive Lori (Shane, not so much).

When Lori died in the Governor's dramatic final siege, Rick was distraught and suffered a nervous breakdown, talking to his dead wife via an unconnected telephone he carried with him. It takes Rick a long time to recover from his wife's death, and this included a short and rather sad relationship with Alexandria Safe-Zone resident Jessie Anderson. When we first met her, Jessie was in an abusive relationship with her husband, Pete. Tensions between the men escalated over Jessie until Rick was forced to kill Pete.

At her instigation, Rick and Jessie began a physical relationship that ended when the community was overrun by walkers and Jessie was dragged into a swarm of the undead. Terrified, she would not let go of Carl and to protect his flesh and blood, Rick severed her hand and Jessie was left to be torn apart with her own son, Ron. Rick and Jessie's partnership never seemed destined to have great longevity, but this was a brutal end to the relationship. Talk about closure!

Season five of AMC's *The Walking Dead* introduced us to both Alexandria and Jessie (as played by Alexandra Breckenridge). Although the spousal abuse storyline was still present, Rick was far more aggressive in his pursuit of her (perhaps finally laying to rest the memory of Lori) and Rick's decision to kill Pete (played superbly by Corey Brill) was a lot more shocking (witness Morgan's look of horror). Jessie is also a stronger and more independent character than the comic's incarnation. With Pete gone, a relationship would seem to be possible for season six, although whether it will play out in the same way is yet to be known.

Rick's current relationship in the comic series is with fellow Atlanta camp survivor, Andrea – a relationship that will never come to pass in the TV version. Rick and Andrea's relationship was long in development. Taking Jessie as an anomaly, Rick is naturally attracted to strong women (there was even some casual flirting with Michonne), and they don't come much stronger than sharpshooter Andrea.

FOR BETTER, FOR WORSE

Andrea's formative experiences were damaging. The loss of her sister to walkers caused extreme trauma. This led to a relationship with Dale, a far older man, who had been married before (to the unseen Erma for 40 years). Andrea's love for Dale was very real, but due to their age difference (at least three decades, if not more – the gap is never mentioned outright) Dale was always cursed by doubt over the relationship and suspected Andrea was only with him out of loyalty and, worse, pity. This dogged their relationship until Dale's death in issue 66. Andrea discovered her talent as a sniper before Dale's passing, but this could be regarded as an unconscious attempt of a damaged individual to enforce isolation upon herself.

"I STILL DON'T APPROVE OF THOSE TWO, BUT ANDREA'S A GROWN WOMAN AND SHE CAN MAKE HER OWN DECISIONS… I'M HAPPY FOR THEM."

DONNA ABOUT ANDREA & DALE

After Dale's death, Andrea had a dalliance with Spencer in the Alexandria Safe-Zone, but she soon broke it off. She realised that she wasn't fully over the death of Dale, and also recognised that as a couple they just weren't very compatible.

Andrea and Rick also had a shaky beginning in romance. After a kiss in issue 96, Rick rejected her, afraid of loving and losing again. The pair officially became an item around issue 98, when Carl found them in bed together. This brought the relationship very much out into the open and they have been together ever since. In the post-'All Out War' era, Andrea has become as much of a community leader as Rick. They are effectively a married couple now.

FATHER AND SON

Perhaps the most lasting relationship in *The Walking Dead* is also the most platonic one: the familial love between father and son, as demonstrated by Rick and Carl Grimes. The bond between these two has seen them through the toughest of times. It has seen them survive the death of loved ones, including wife/mother and daughter/sister. And even when tested – when Carl fears that his father has succumbed to illness or when Rick fears for his son's life after he gets shot through the eye socket – their support of each other has got them through to the other side.

With Carl currently hitting his difficult teenage years (when hormones run rife) and Rick under huge pressure as the leader of a thriving community, cracks may begin to appear in their relationship. But, inarguably, it's clear that they would still do anything to help each other, including sacrifice themselves. And you can't get much of a stronger relationship than that.

FOR RICHER, FOR POORER

Michonne is a mysterious character due to the emotional distance that she keeps around herself. This may be a defense mechanism of sorts, a complement to the cold steel of her signature katana's blade, but it extends to her relationships, too.

When Michonne arrived outside the prison in issue 19, she appeared as a lone, hooded figure dragging two neutered walkers in chains. She had removed their lower jaws and arms, impairing their ability to attack and was using them as cover to pass unscathed through the wilds. The zombies are jokingly referred to as her 'boyfriends,' but as we discovered in the Michonne special, one of these zombies really was her pre-apocalypse boyfriend, Mike, which is revealed more directly in the TV show's episode 'Try.'

MORGAN!

I'M OKAY-- I'M--

Most characters in *The Walking Dead* cannot bear to be near zombified loved ones. Exceptions to this usually signify a character being emotionally disturbed (such as Morgan Jones' inability to dispatch his undead son, Duane, and the Governor keeping his undead daughter in his home). Michonne does not seem to be struggling with a mental illness more severe than anyone else, given the situation, but she is certainly a troubled character. Increasingly she has difficulty reconciling her skills as a warrior, and the value these are given by her group, with her growing desire for a normal life. Her intimate relationships demonstrate her inner conflicts.

She played a key role in breaking up a relationship between Tyreese and Carol in the comic, seducing Tyreese (who was not an unwilling participant). The couple eventually moved into a

cell together, leading to the rapid deterioration of Carol's mental wellbeing and ultimately her death. In the comic, Carol was a weak character who stayed that way. She defined herself through relationships with partners who were either ambivalent or hostile towards her. Her husband was abusive, Tyreese unfaithful, and when she formed an attachment to Lori, it was roughly rebuffed. Carol was a personality in need of constant support and affirmation. This led to her growing mental instability and, in the end, her suicide. As for Michonne and Tyreese's relationship, this was brought to an abrupt end when he was murdered by the Governor in issue 46. Michonne herself finally put the risen Tyreese down with her blade just a few issues later.

Her next relationship was with Morgan Jones. Having struggled with mental illness since the death of his son, Morgan confided in

I CAN LIVE WITH POTENTIAL. POTENTIAL HAS PROMISE.

I CAN WORK WITH POTENTIAL.

GOOD, NOW GO DOWNSTAIRS AND MAKE SURE YOUR STUPID TIGER DIDN'T TEAR APART MY BATHROOM.

I'LL MAKE COFFEE.

HAREM KEEPER

The comic series' first big human villain, the Governor, was a brutal rapist. After assaulting Michonne, his ability to attack women was definitively removed by her later in the story. The second of the great human antagonists, Negan, appears to be in stark contrast to the Governor in his stated abhorrence of sexual violence. However, look further into Negan and it becomes apparent that he is just as abusive, but he goes about it in a far more devious way, using his power to engineer a situation where women submit to him 'willingly,' allowing him to keep a harem of beautiful lovers.

Whether Negan actually gains pleasure from his abuse is unclear. What is very evident is that the real object of his enforcement of sexual dominance is not to control women but to mentally castrate their men. Negan subjugates women in order to establish his alpha male status. He is an animal marking his territory, a lion dominating his pride.

Michonne his feelings of guilt and despair. Michonne was less than sympathetic, but after Morgan's death, she told Rick that she really did want to make a life with him. It may well be that in suppressing her own guilt, Michonne could not abide seeing it accepted by others. Morgan was also put to final rest after rising from the dead by Michonne. How does the song go? You always hurt the ones you love...

Michonne's most recent relationship to date is with the Kingdom's leader, Ezekiel. The relationship started badly, with Michonne not taking well to Ezekiel's regal airs and graces. However, it developed into intitially a physical relationship. There are signs that Michonne is moving forward here. She was instrumental in forcing Ezekiel to rise up to take on the responsibilities of his position when the conflict with the Saviors escalated. Also, she hasn't killed him, either undead or alive (yet).

IN SICKNESS AND IN HEALTH

The relationship between Tyreese's teenage daughter, Julie, and her boyfriend, Chris, was one of the most tragically dysfunctional in the whole of *The Walking Dead* storyline. Already an item when Tyreese's group met Rick's in issue seven, Julie and Chris kept their relationship secret, knowing that Julie's father would very much disapprove. Even in the relative spaciousness of the prison, the pair found it difficult to consummate their relationship. Chris decided they should kill each other, and Julie is pressured into a suicide pact. Why or how the idea came about, we can't say, but it was probably based on adolescent notions of romance. The pair were meant to shoot each other, but Chris fired first, killing Julie. Tyreese in turn killed Chris, and then very deliberately waited for him to turn so he could do it again.

> "IT WASN'T SUPPOSED TO BE LIKE THIS. WE WERE SUPPOSED TO BE TOGETHER FOREVER."
> **CHRIS ABOUT JULIE**

THREESOMES

The relationship between Eugene, Rosita and Abraham is a very interesting one, much of it based on survival. Initially, Abe and Rosita are together, with Eugene very much the third wheel. The latter is clearly very jealous that his much beefier companion is sleeping with this beautiful woman (he even spies on them when they have sex), and on paper, they are a strong couple. But it is soon revealed that Abraham was simply using Rosita for companionship as he worked through his troubles over the death of his ex-wife and children. As soon as Abraham meets Holly in Alexandria, there's an immediate sexual attraction between the two, and he drops Rosita like a stone in water.

Eugene is furious with Abraham, but he also realizes this is his chance to court Rosita. She's initially resistant, but eventually (as we discover after the time jump in issue 127) she does fall for Eugene's charms. Clearly, problems exist in their relationship, which has begun to go cold two years down the line, but whether this is because Rosita still remains hurt by Abraham's rejection remains to be seen. Is she with Eugene for the same reason Abraham was with her? For companionship alone? Time will tell…

"I WANT [ROSITA] TO BE HAPPY WITHOUT ME. LIKE I AM WITHOUT HER. I JUST WANT THINGS TO BE RIGHT. IF SHE CAN BE HAPPY WITH YOU, GREAT."
ABRAHAM TO EUGENE

TO LOVE AND TO CHERISH

Maggie Greene and Glenn share one of the strongest and most touching relationships in both the comic and TV incarnations of *The Walking Dead*. Their relationship began as a casual one (at least for Maggie), but despite obstacles getting in their way – such as the initial objections of Maggie's father, Hershel, her struggles with severe depression, and (in the comic) her attempted suicide – Maggie and Glenn are one of the rare examples of a couple who married post-apocalypse.

In the comic series, after Glenn is murdered by Negan, Maggie does not lose herself in grief. The relationship has made her a stronger person. Pregnant with Glenn's child at the time, this gave her another reason to live.

Maggie goes on to become the leader of the Hilltop community (and gives birth to baby Hershel), but despite some enthusiastic suitors (including Dante), even two years after Glenn's death, Maggie shows no interest in pursuing a relationship with someone new.

I THEE WORSHIP

The relationship of Aaron and Eric is notable as a positive portrayal of a gay relationship, avoiding clichés common in many mainstream dramas. In both comic and television incarnations, Aaron is a character who is not defined by his sexuality. The character is established, allowed to be heroic in combat, and shown to be a very capable and intelligent individual before it is revealed he is gay. Aaron's partner Eric is a softer and gentler person, but as a couple they have proven to be just as caring and concerned for each other as with any heterosexual relationship. Indeed, in many ways their relationship seems much stronger than many of the others we see in *The Walking Dead*. When Eric is martyred in battle (in the comic book) in issue 118, Aaron's grief is moving and his retribution severe.

At its heart, *The Walking Dead* is a story about people and what it means to be alive. In the variety and depth of the relationships between the characters it seems to ask, without intimacy, is there any reason to be alive? Naturally, this is not limited to sexual intimacy – the bonds of friendship, kinship and blood are also strong, but *The Walking Dead* is an expression of the power of love to light a candle in the most oppressive darkness. •

CHOICE CUTS

GLENN

Having examined the 'Choice Cuts' of Maggie, it seemed only fitting to feature her husband in our 'Choice Cuts' selection too: Glenn. A stalwart of the comic for 99 issues, Glenn remains one of *TWDM*'s favorite characters, and we're still bitter he's no longer around. So here are some of our favorite Glenn moments from during his run, as well as the final event from that fateful issue #100.
WORDS: Rich Matthews

PAYMENT ON DELIVERY

Be careful what you wish for, you just might get it...

Before the dead started to walk, Glenn was up to his eyes in debt. The pizza delivery boy was in way over his head and was about to lose everything (his apartment, car and so on) with no hope in sight. Estranged from his family, he stole cars while at college just to keep his head above water.

When faced with having to crawl back to his parents, cap in hand, he wished for a miracle to get him out of his seemingly doomed situation. Then the dead started to walk...

Suddenly, his previous existence of living on a knife's edge became the norm for everyone, so Glenn was better prepared than most; his tolerance for stress and honed gift for quick thinking under extreme pressure turned into a massive bonus in this changed world. As did his ability to hotwire cars and sneak about undetected.

In a weird way, like so many of his fellow survivors, Glenn seemed to be made for the apocalypse, and he clearly viewed the new order as a giant reset button that gave him his second chance. And he grabbed that chance with both hands – wife, children, and responsibility. He was needed and appreciated.

Alas, the new world has no interest in intent, honor or respect, and Glenn's ultimate fate was cruelly beyond his control.

HELPING HAND

Glenn couldn't have made a bigger splash in his debut in issue #2 – Rick is dead meat, destined to be the zombie dessert that follows the main meal of his horse, until Glenn yanks the hapless sheriff out of a horde of encroaching walkers, up onto the roofs of Atlanta where they make a dash to safety. It's Glenn who explains to Rick the extent of the apocalypse, how to avoid the walkers, and what to do in a pinch, then offers him refuge with the ragtag group he's become a part of. Which is where Rick is reunited with Lori and Carl.

Yes, other characters have made more dramatic first appearances – Michonne, Ezekiel, Negan and so on – but no one has had as big an impact on the story as Glenn. In a nutshell, no Glenn, no Rick, no comic.

"I CAN GET YOU OUT OF HERE. FOLLOW ME." GLENN'S FIRST WORDS

TRUE ROMANCE

Glenn's crush on Maggie began back at Hershel's farm. Typically, though, the young scavenger's shyness almost got in the way of one of *The Walking Dead*'s greatest romances – which actually led to the comic book's first wedding. And while it was lust that first (and finally) got them together, the depth of Glenn's feelings were truly tested first at the farm, with the slaughter of Maggie's turned family in the barn; then in the prison, ahead of the Governor's attack (ultimately, the pair decided to leave Rick and the group behind); and then Maggie's suicide attempt on the road to Washington.

While he was genuinely rocked by Maggie's near-hanging, in the end it was the making of their relationship – not only because he saved her life by stopping Abraham from finishing her off until they were certain she was dead, but also because it made the pair realize and examine what they meant to each other. Beyond the obvious physical connection and the enforced parental bond introduced by their adopted child Sophia's attachment to Maggie, it's apparent they meant a great deal to each other. Their relationship had a chance to be fully formalized when Glenn found out that Maggie was pregnant with his child, even if biological parenthood would sadly elude him.

> "I LOVE YOU – NOT THAT FLIRTY GIRL I MET AT THE FARM HOUSE, NOT THAT SEX MACHINE I LIVED WITH AT THE PRISON – YOU. EVERY FLAW, EVERY QUIRK..." GLENN TO MAGGIE

FAN FAVORITE

Glenn was one of the most fearless characters in the series. That doesn't mean he felt no fear – he most certainly did, especially when his family was involved – but when something needed doing, Glenn would step up to the plate. This often put him at odds with Maggie, who sometimes accused him of being reckless, but without Glenn many of the characters would not have survived as long as they did.

One of his bravest moments came when he chose to help a stranded Andrea during the walker attack on Alexandria. Glenn, Heath and Spencer traverse a flimsy-looking suspended rope above a horde of hungry mouths, providing the 'No Way Out' storyline with one of its best covers (issue #81, a personal favorite of *TWDM*).

It's actions like these that made Glenn a favorite with fans. No wonder there was such uproar when the landmark issue #100 came around – no one was expecting Kirkman to kill Glenn off. That it was done in such a brutal way too, over several pages, caused uproar among the fans who inundated the comic's 'Letter Hacks' section with letters of outrage and complaint. We've only just about forgiven him ourselves...

THE GAME PLAN

Glenn is one of only three characters to have appeared in the comic, the television series and the video game, but can you name the other two (see end of this section for the answer)? Glenn meets Lee and Clementine in Telltale Games' playable version of *The Walking Dead* in the first episode of the series, 'A New Day.' Glenn has been living and working at his pizza job in Macon and first meets Lee in the latter's family pharmacy. He helps Lee and Carley to save a trapped survivor in a motel, before heading off to Atlanta where presumably he would run into Shane, Lori, and Carl, before rescuing Rick from a hungry zombie horde. He's voiced in the game by a Telltale senior cinematic artist, Nick Herman.

Oh, and the two other characters to appear in comic, TV show and game: Shawn and Hershel Greene.

POSITIVE PARENTING

If you need evidence that the apocalypse was the making of Glenn, just look to his decision to step up and be Sophia's surrogate father after her mother, Carol, committed suicide. Admittedly, this was in part because Sophia buried all memory of her mother deep inside her unconscious and seemed to imprint on Maggie as her 'new mom.' And Glenn only really became obviously paternal towards Sophia after Maggie's suicide attempt, making sure the young girl understood that neither of them would leave her – a slightly questionable promise in the world of *The Walking Dead*, but a kind one nonetheless.

Sophia was destined to suffer even more trauma as a witness – clutched in Maggie's desperate embrace – to Glenn's horrific bludgeoning by Negan. But prior to the tragic events of issue #100, it was Glenn and Maggie's love and support that managed to help Sophia get back on an even keel. Although it was never overtly stated that she remembers Carol, she did refer to Glenn and Maggie as her adoptive parents in issue #72, a reality that Sophia had previously seemed to spurn in favor of the fantasy that they were her actual parents.

However, just stop and think of the man Glenn was when he first appeared in issue #2, the devil-may-care scavenger with an almost foolhardy willingness to venture back into the city to grab whatever the camp needed, inventively playing chicken with all manner of walkers. By the time he met his maker, he would have never taken such risks as the main provider for Maggie and Sophia. He may not have been the toughest, but at the time of his death, Glenn was one of the most valuable, reliable and socially conscious members of Rick's group. Which is why it hurt even more...

"YOU WANT HER OUT OF HER SHELL, LIVING A HAPPY LIFE... THEN WE NEED TO MOVE TO THE HILLTOP. TRUST ME." GLENN MAKES A FATEFUL DECISION

KOREA MOVE

One of the best things about the world as portrayed in *The Walking Dead* is that race, sexuality and gender no longer seem to matter. The survivors have more to worry about than the color of someone's skin, who fancies whom, or what the contents of someone's underwear is. Racism and sexism still exist, but only in some of the less likable characters, but for most it's just not an issue.

Take Glenn's Korean heritage for example, it's not really mentioned and has no real bearing on the way his character is developed. Indeed, its most noticeable reference is in issue #100 when Negan states he doesn't want to kill an Asian man for fear of being called racist – not that it ultimately stops him from doing the deed.

GLENN FACT FILE

NAME: Glenn **AGE:** 22-24 estimated (comic) **PLAYED IN SERIES BY:** Steven Yeun

JOB: Pizza delivery boy (pre-apocalypse); supply runner (post-apocalypse)

RELATIONSHIPS POST-APOCALYPSE: Maggie (wife)

LIKES: Maggie Greene (wife), Sophia (adopted daughter), Hershel Greene (unborn son); the Greene family (all dead) – Hershel (father-in-law), Arnold and Billy (brothers-in-law), Rachel, Susie, and Lacey (sisters-in-law), but maybe not Shawn (brother-in-law)

FIRST APPEARANCE: Issue #2

CURRENT STATUS: Deceased

WELL, WELL!

In the TV iteration, Glenn is brilliantly played by relative newcomer Steven Yeun. Although similar to his comic book version, Glenn is a little more confident in the show. This is demonstrated on many occasions but nowhere better than when he entered the dark train tunnel in search of Maggie in season four's 'Us.'

However, probably *TWDM*'s favorite Glenn moment comes from 'Cherokee Rose' and could have been taken right out of the early days of the comic book: he bravely allows himself to be lowered down into a well to hook a rope around a trapped (and very bloated) walker. Having survived that, and with the zombie tied off, he helps the others haul it up, only for the thing to split in half and spill bilged gore everywhere. Nice!

A DEATH IN THE FAMILY

Trying desperately to find a grain of positivity from a vast desert of horror, Glenn did at least have a memorable end, shuffling off this mortal coil in an image that is hard to wipe from the mind's eye, no matter how much you want to get rid of the gruesome memory.

When Glenn discovered that Maggie was pregnant, he made a decision that they would all be much safer as a family living at Hilltop because of Rick's war against the Saviors and Negan. This turned out to be a fateful choice.

During an expedition to Hilltop – where Rick intends to recruit Jesus and his people, and Glenn will prepare for relocation – the group of survivors are ambushed by a vengeful Negan. Bitter about the murder of his bandit team, Negan decides that he needs to send a strong, clear message to Rick and the other survivors in the area.

Thus, Glenn is lined up with his fellow captives while Negan portentously announces that one of them must die as retribution for all the Saviors that have been killed. He then brutally beats Glenn to death with the barb-wire-wrapped baseball bat that he calls Lucille.

Glenn's final word was an attempt to say "Maggie," even though his skull was caved-in and one of his eyes was hanging free from the crushed socket. Even when dead, Negan continues to beat Glenn's corpse, literally reducing the body to a pulp. But at least Glenn wouldn't rise and need to be killed again. Small mercy.

Maggie took his remains to Hilltop where she honored his last wishes, and settled there with Sophia to have her baby and live as a family. It's ironic (and sad) that the walkers never appeared to pose a threat to Glenn; his problems came from the living. He was always in the most danger because of other people's plays for power and petty vengeance. •

"PLEASE. PLEASE DON'T. M...M...M...M...MAG...MAGGIE!" GLENN'S FINAL WORDS

MARCH TO WAR

The knives are out in this edition of our examination of specific storylines of *The Walking Dead*. Glenn has been murdered, the survivor colonies are at breaking point and Savior Negan has repeatedly given Rick a lesson in leadership and tactics as we open the pages of volume 19, 'March To War.' With the epic 'All Out War' just six issues away, this prelude volume sees the war drums starting to be struck as the bugle rallies the troops. WORDS: Yvonne M Jones

It happens to the best of long-running comic series. An issue or volume lingers longer on character than plot, and some readers lob low-level digs like 'filler' and 'nothing really happens' at the series' writers with abandon. However, others, still catching their breath after back-to-back tragedies and action set piece-packed issues, appreciate the pacing. And they don't begrudge their favorite characters a time-out as long as the story doesn't suffer.

Readers leafing through the first half of volume 19 of *The Walking Dead*, 'March To War,' might be forgiven for writing it off as a placeholder. Subdued scenes – such as the recently widowed Maggie's prenatal exam – promise a significant respite before, true to the volume's title, the build-up to war escalates as the volume comes to its conclusion.

The previous arc, the high-octane 'What Comes After,' saw Rick following through on his plan to lull the series' newest villain Negan, a baseball bat-wielding sociopath who

> Subdued scenes promise a significant respite before the build-up to war escalates as the volume concludes.

is the group's first substantial threat since the Governor, into complacency. Rick has *seemingly* convinced Negan that the Alexandria Safe-Zone will submit to routine Savior plunder, something he characteristically neglected to mention to the Alexandria residents until he felt he absolutely must. Rick concludes that when Negan is vulnerable, Rick and his makeshift army will attack and bring an end to the tyrant's reign of terror once and for all.

However, Rick's apparent capitulation sat badly with Carl, who snuck into Negan's stronghold and killed as many Saviors as his ammunition allowed. Rather than retaliate by ending his life, Carl's

PARDON THE INTRUSION, YOUNG LADY.

I JUST THOUGHT I'D DO MY PART TO PROVIDE REASSURANCE IN THE CAPABLE HANDS OF DOCTOR HARLAN CARSON.

MAN'S A *MIRACLE* WORKER.

The characteristics and values necessary to lead are a core element to the storyline of 'March To War.'

a Hilltop ally, if she suspects Gregory of alerting Negan to Rick's plan. She agrees, but Rick doesn't entirely convince his Alexandria comrades, Andrea, Spencer Monroe, or Michonne, that his plan of action is sound. As both the group's resident hawk and now Rick's lover, Andrea is in, despite her doubts. But Spencer's opinion is clouded by the resentment he still carries after his late father handed the Safe-Zone leadership to Rick. As for Michonne, she is weary of being deployed to execute schemes she has no say in. The series' most fierce warrior flatly admits that she's tired and can't bring herself to care.

They all resent this latest evidence of Rick's unilateral decision-making. Only Carl – still charged from his own assault on the Savior stronghold – supports his father wholeheartedly.

Jesus grows suspicious when Kal takes off on a mysterious perimeter check before a scheduled meeting. He follows on horseback and catches up with him at a literal and metaphorical crossroads. Kal soon realizes Jesus and Rick aren't the warmongers he imagined, but he has other reasons for blowing their cover. "You can't decide this for all of us," he protests. "You can't drag us to war without getting everyone onboard."

Rick's absolute rule is a note writer Robert Kirkman hits again and again throughout the series, but it has slightly more weight coming from a character who isn't one of Rick's insiders. Ultimately, Kal decides to throw in with Rick simply because he hates living under Negan's boot more than he mistrusts Rick.

Rick convinces more than 20 men and women from the Safe-Zone – including Carl, Andrea, Heath, and a now more amenable Michonne – to join him on a supply run that's really a covert combat training boot camp held at Ezekiel's Kingdom. Michonne greets Ezekiel's Knights of the Round Table-style theatrics with her katana's sharp blade and bloodshed is narrowly averted. So is a mauling from Ezekiel's pet tiger, Shiva. It's a sign that nothing is quite what it seems in Ezekiel's Kingdom.

Later, Michonne slips out for a moment of respite in the Kingdom's vegetable garden as the rest of the survivors dine on roasted boar. When Ezekiel follows, he gets a piece of her mind. He admits to her he was just a pre-apocalypse zookeeper and

assassination attempt *moved* Negan in some sick way, and so he shocked everyone by returning the boy to Rick unharmed. Jesus then decided it was time for Rick to form an alliance with Ezekiel, the leader of a neighboring survivor colony who also hates Negan. And so, on to this story…

The opening pages of 'March to War' find a pregnant Maggie settling uneasily into life at the Hilltop with her adopted daughter Sophia. She's quiet with grief, but visiting Glenn's grave three times a day helps. Or it does until Brianna, a chatty stranger, mentions that the Hilltop's besotted leader Gregory bent the rules to allow Maggie to bury Glenn and not burn him.

Never the most likable of male characters in *The Walking Dead*, even for Gregory this is a new low. Maggie's murdered husband is still warm in the ground, and yet Gregory's already laying the groundwork to make a move on her. It's yet another sign of weakness in Gregory's leadership – which will raise its ugly head in the following volumes – and one is left wondering how he ever became the colony's leader at all. He couldn't be more different than Rick if he tried. The characteristics and values necessary to lead are a core element to the storyline of 'March To War' as we are introduced to both the best and worst aspects of Rick's command, and a new authority figure in the shape of Ezekiel (first introduced in issue 108) emerges.

Elsewhere, Rick is still hoping to avenge Glenn's brutal murder by Negan, and sends Jesus to speak with Maggie. He asks her to contact Kal,

> ## Rick's absolute rule is a note writer Robert Kirkman hits again and again throughout the series.

IN A NUTSHELL

TITLE: March To War
FEATURED ISSUES: 109-114
COLLECTION: Volume 19
SYNOPSIS: After learning more about the Saviors' base from his son, Rick decides to put his plan into action by uniting the forces of the Kingdom, the Hilltop and Alexandria against the tyrannical rule of Negan. However, not all of his 'followers' can be wholly trusted, and Negan has plans of his own, turning up at Alexandria unexpectedly while Rick was rallying forces at the Kingdom. When Negan kills Spencer Monroe, Rick jumps the gun and tries to end the conflict there and then, but he once again underestimates his nemesis. Negan is proving to be an unpredictable and canny opponent. All out war is inevitable…

TIDBITS:

- Spencer is the only major loss this volume, although given his dislike and attempted double-cross of Rick, perhaps his death is not such a loss after all.

- We learn much more about Ezekiel this volume, but more importantly, the romantic seeds between the former zookeeper and Michonne are also sown. This has developed into an element of the current story that has been frustrating fans of the comic ever since issue 127. Where are Zeke and Michonne? Are they still together? Are they still in the Kingdom? Fingers crossed we'll find out soon.

- The cover for issue 114, depicting Jesus putting the boot in to some Saviors, happens to be one of *TWDM*'s favorites. Go, Jesus, go!

- This volume has the least walkers of any of the series to date. Indeed, issues 109, 110 and 114 do not feature any walking dead at all.

> "People want someone to follow. Makes them feel safe." Ezekiel

community theater geek who nursed a sick tiger back to health. He doesn't have a 'god complex,' just a love of theatrics, but why complain when his people weaved the threads of his life into an origin story befitting the king they both needed and wanted?

"People want someone to follow," Ezekiel explains, as much to himself as to the reader, who must sometimes wonder how Rick, the Governor, and certainly the likes of Gregory maintain rule. "Makes them feel safe."

Ezekiel also proves that he's astute, noting that Michonne is "playing samurai" the same way he's playing king. Michonne's perpetual frown softens into a smile as she entertains the thought that Ezekiel is courting, not conning, her. When was the last time Michonne was seen as a woman worthy of courtesy, and not merely a paranoid but skilled soldier? It's a welcome fleshing-out of Ezekiel's character too, giving him a depth missing from his eccentric bluster since his introduction. A sense of doubt still remains over his motives, but in this moment of quiet at least he does seem genuine, and more human.

The next day, after Rick and Andrea train their motley crew of soldiers in hand-to-hand combat and gunplay, Rick admits there's too much about Negan and the Saviors they don't know. The Saviors never seem to carry many guns, and they don't know for sure how many Hilltop recruits Jesus can muster, how many Saviors reside at the group's outposts, or how many outposts they even have.

Their questions are moot. Miles away, Negan, his barbed wire-wrapped baseball bat, Lucille, and the Saviors arrive at the Alexandria Safe-Zone gates demanding tribute several days early. And Kirkman makes sure the action comes fast enough to induce papercuts in any reader who flipped ponderously through the volume's opening pages.

The following scenes highlight just how erratic a villain Negan is, demonstrating his venomous sense of humor. Not necessarily smart in an intellectual way, he is one heckuva of a poker player and, as this bold move proves, he should never be underestimated. We still know very little about his background, which doesn't compromise his entertainment value in the least. But it contributes to his lack of nuance. Negan also shows some interest, though not a need, in being seen as a reasonable man of purpose as well as a dangerous one. His leadership style is one based on power; he has it in abundance and is not afraid to use it to intimidate others.

When Rick, Andrea, and others return to the Safe-Zone, they learn that Spencer made a deadly mistake. In Rick's absence, Spencer described him as an ego-driven maniac who doesn't play well with others, and suggested that Negan should kill Rick, letting Spencer himself replace him as the Safe-Zone's new leader.

Once again, Negan's unpredictability comes to the fore. He has either fallen for Rick's feigned submission or just respected it, whereas Spencer's attempt to double-cross Rick is, he

OH, HOW EMBARRASSING! THERE THEY ARE!

THEY WERE INSIDE YOU THE WHOLE TIME.

YOU *DID* HAVE GUTS. I'VE NEVER BEEN SO *WRONG* BEFORE IN MY LIFE!

Negan faces a familiar leadership dilemma: killing Rick will make him a martyr, but letting him live could prove costly.

considers, underhanded. "I think about you, Spencer, the guy who waited until Rick was gone to sneak over… to get me to do his dirty work so that he could take Rick's place," he explains before jamming a knife into Spencer's mid-section. Or maybe Spencer's description of Rick sounded a little too familiar and Negan was annoyed that Spencer didn't see the irony.

Rick makes a poorly thought-out decision as Negan and the Saviors prepare to drive away. "Negan's here with about eight guys," he blurts to a startled Andrea. "This might be our best chance to get him. He's not leaving here alive."

Within minutes, Andrea is in sniper position in the bell tower. Carl and every available sharpshooter in the Safe-Zone are lined up at the wall near the gate. And two Saviors are dead as Negan dives for cover. Then more shots ring out, one of them knocking a pistol out of Rick's hand.

Again, Negan proves he's not an idiot, having placed well-armed Saviors throughout the surrounding area before showing his face at Alexandria's gates. Negan reveals his visits to pick up offerings are often early or late to give him leeway to arrange a back-up crew for ambushes just like this.

With Rick helpless, it's Andrea who is in real trouble. Her shots have given away her position, and after a savage battle with a Savior lackey, the Savior puts down his blade to choke her to death with what almost reads as genuine sorrow. He's much sorrier when she grabs the blade and slashes his throat before pushing him over the bell tower's ledge.

Down at the gates, Negan faces a familiar leadership dilemma. Killing Rick will make him a martyr to his people, but letting him live could prove costly. He eventually decides that he must break Rick, and the best way he can do that is by killing the three closest Safe-Zone residents, "like I did your Asian friend." Then he says he will go over the wall and kill Carl for shooting a hole in his beloved Lucille.

As Negan begins to play 'Eeny Meeny Miny Moe' with the group's lives, Jesus arrives and dodges an array of Savior bullets

because, as he tells Negan, "your soldiers suck." He quickly takes Negan hostage after smashing him in the face with Lucille. Negan tries to reason his way out of the chokehold as both his men and Rick's hold their fire. They have reached an impasse that doesn't bode well for anyone.

Then, like Chekhov's gun (a dramatic principle that requires every element in a story to be 'necessary', with everything else removed), Shiva the tiger attacks. Ezekiel and the rest of his small army follow behind, and chaos ensues. Negan and the Saviors who weren't mauled by Shiva run for their trucks as Ezekiel gives the order to gun them down. But it's just for show.

"We have to go after them," Rick screams. "We can't let them regroup."

Ezekiel, who may already have eclipsed Rick as the most rational decision maker and tactician in the story, disagrees. He explains that Negan's forces outnumber their own and that their recent success was simply because they caught Negan with his britches down. It's a sentiment Michonne echoes as Dr Cloyd tends to Rick and Andrea. "You threw away our advantage," she tells Rick ominously. "He knows what's coming now."

Rick, ever the post-apocalyptic optimist, still thinks they can burn Negan and the Saviors down to the ground in a

day or two, three at the most. But, as Jesus notes later on, Rick's most recent actions were not his finest hour.

Unlike many themes in *The Walking Dead*, which are often woven into many layers of storyline, Kirkman takes the opportunity to directly address the qualities needed for good leadership, using Jesus as his explanatory mouthpiece. Gregory abuses his power, just wanting an easy life at the Hilltop. Ezekiel remains an enigma hidden behind a fantasy at this point: we know a little more about him, sure, but he's still mostly a mystery. Negan is Genghis Khan, ruling by the rod (or baseball bat). Meanwhile Rick makes mistakes, but his intentions remain pure, and that inspires people to fight for what's right, and, as Jesus says, "right now, we can't get that anywhere else... You're a leader we can follow," Jesus affirms, evoking his namesake as he grasps Rick by the shoulders under a vivid sun.

Miles away, his tail between his legs, a livid Negan orders his Saviors to follow him into war. The march to war is over. Now the real battle begins. •

MAKING A SPLASH

One of the highlights of Charlie Adlard's artwork is his tremendous splash panels (aka full-page or double-page illustrations). Although he uses these splash panels relatively minimally, when he does do them, they are always memorable. *TWDM* looks at our choice of one of his most impactful splashes to feature in the comic.

WORDS: Dan Auty

HOW DID WE GET HERE?

This splash appears in issue 96. Rick gives an impassioned speech to Andrea, Carl, Glenn, and Michonne, explaining why he has agreed to join the Hilltop and help the residents in their fight against Negan and the Saviors. "I see a world without roamers… a world where we don't have to be scared anymore," he tells them.

WHAT'S THE SCENE?

Rick stands with his back to us on the road that leads away from the colony. Carl is beside him, while Andrea, Glenn, and Michonne stand watching and listening. Behind them, the early morning sunlight spills over the horizon.

WORDS AND PICTURES

Adlard's splashes are often widescreen visual treats that allow the artist to deliver a moment of dramatic impact. However, this splash is a static dialogue scene more akin to the standard multiframe design.

THE FUTURE IS BRIGHT…

The characters take up less than half the image, the rest is occupied by the landscape. The visual metaphor is clear: as Rick explains why the Hilltop colony could mean a new start, the road winds away behind them into a hopeful sunrise. Retrospectively, this moment is packed with pathos, and a little irony; four issues later, we will see just how wrong Rick is… •

THE SECRET DIARY OF A WALKER

It's not easy being a zombie in *The Walking Dead* world, as our week in the life/death of an undead walker shows. Diary entries transcribed by Dan Auty…

MONDAY

It's been a quiet few months, but I'm hopin' business picks up soon. A lot of my buddies have left their old jobs and moved on to new things — eating, lumbering, rotting, that kinda thing — but I'm stayin' put at the gas station. Fillin' gas tanks is my life.

TUESDAY

A bunch of normos drove by, and started takin' gas from the working pump. When I realized they weren't gonna be payin' me I came out after them, but there ain't much meat left on my leg and I can't run much no more. Those darn normos took off when they saw me. Folks ain't got no respect!

WEDNESDAY

Jawless Billy came by to chew the fat and sink a few cold ones. Billy ended up gettin' it all over his overalls on account of him not havin' a jaw no more. No Legs Hank and Stumpy Joe are still stayin' with me.

I Just can't get them boys to leave, no matter how hard I hint.

THURSDAY

Shut up early today — no customers at all and I'm low on gas, ever since my ol' lady sprayed it over herself. Dang, but she went up fast!

FRIDAY

Me and some of the guys were hangin' out when this normo came runnin' outta the woods, dressed in some kinda funny-lookin'

suit. He was headin' for this ol' Ford that I know ain't been driven for months. I figured he might want to buy some gas, so I started up after him. I guess he thought I wanted to eat him, but honest to god, I wouldn't chow down on nobody until I made sure their tank was full. That's just the kinda guy I am! •

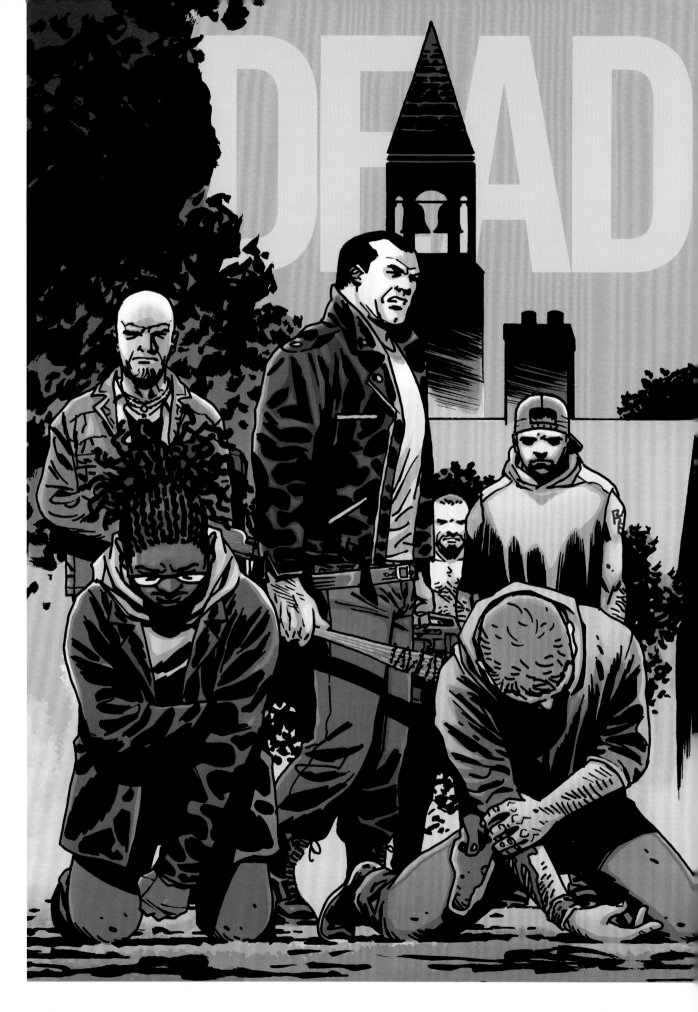

RECKONING

If there's one inevitability of life it's that death will come to us all one day. There are many ways to bite the dust in *The Walking Dead* world (biting dust actually isn't one of them), so *TWDM* thought it wise to spare a thought to those who have been left pushing up the daisies in the comic book series, revealing how they died and why. WORDS: Dan Auty

I can be both a comfort and a drawback of much genre fiction – whether television, movies or on the printed page – knowing that in most cases the heroes are not going to die. Sure, central characters might undergo all sorts of terrible experiences along the way, and occasionally one might die to raise the stakes a little. But the chances are that whoever you thought would survive until the end does just that.

From the very start, *The Walking Dead* has gone out of its way to subvert this, ensuring that the characters that most evoke our sympathies are in no less danger than its villains or minor characters. This has long been one of its biggest strengths – the constant threat that looms over every member of Robert Kirkman's ensemble ensures that the comic remains as gripping now as it did 10 years ago. Even the title signifies the possibility that the clock is ticking on every character. Being the hero is no protection either, as Kirkman himself has confirmed to *Daily Dead*: "Yeah, Rick could go at any time."

THE WALKING DEAD FOCUSES ON THE LENGTHS PEOPLE WILL GO TO KEEP THEMSELVES ALIVE, WHICH INEVITABLY RESULTS IN CONFLICT AND KILLING.

Death, of course, comes in many forms, and *The Walking Dead* is not just a zombie comic. It is primarily a drama about survival, and just as many notable deaths have resulted from contact with other humans as they have from encounters with the undead. The series focuses time and time again on the lengths that people will go to keep themselves alive, which, in a world where food and safe shelter is scarce and only the strongest survive, inevitably results in conflict and killing.

So let's take a look at some of the ways to meet your maker…

IN THE BEGINNING...

In the earliest issues, it was more the zombies than other humans that provided the immediate threat. This was before society had completely broken down, and survivors were much more likely to work alongside each other than against; that now-familiar instinct to mistrust all strangers was yet to set in. Kirkman was careful not to kill off too many characters in the first few issues, and when he did, it had a far more shocking effect than it would a decade later.

The first human death of any consequence – in other words, a character we had known over several issues – was Amy in issue five, attacked by zombies in the woodland camp where the survivors first gathered. The response to her demise from her friends was powerful, and she was afforded a funeral, something that would soon become a rarity.

Similarly, Jim, another member of the group who lasted only a few issues, is the first to die from infection. At this stage, the group aren't even sure that he will return once he goes, so recent is the zombie outbreak.

THE RESPONSE TO AMY'S DEMISE WAS POWERFUL, AND SHE WAS AFFORDED A FUNERAL, SOMETHING THAT WOULD SOON BECOME A RARITY.

WALKER CHOW!

As *The Walking Dead* story continues, the characters become better equipped to cope with flesh-hungry zombies – they learn how to deal with them in varying numbers, what to do to avoid detection and so on.

But walker attacks continue, and although many of the most significant deaths occur in different ways, Kirkman never lets his characters – or readers – become complacent as to their threat. Every empty building or closed door could house a zombie, and some of the series' most shocking deaths have resulted from sudden and unexpected walker attacks. Donna, for instance, bitten in the face as she opens a door of a supposedly abandoned house; Dale, his arm munched during a routine mission (leading to his encounter with the Hunters and subsequent euthanasia at the hands of Andrea); or more recently, Alexandria survivor John, suddenly overwhelmed by zombies while hiding from the Saviors. Characters that we have lived with for dozens of issues – Morgan,

DRIVEN TO THE POINT OF DESPAIR BY THE REJECTION OF THE TWO PEOPLE CLOSEST TO HER, CAROL COMMITS SUICIDE BY OFFERING HERSELF TO A WALKER.

savaged by walkers while trying to clear Alexandria alongside Rick – could be dispatched with absolutely no warning or build-up.

The Walking Dead is not a comic to shy away from the dark and the subversive, and some of the zombie deaths are far weirder than simply being chomped on by a hungry ghoul. Soon after the introduction of the Greene family, Hershel's second eldest son, Arnold, becomes zombie chow at the teeth of his own brother Shawn, one of the re-animated family members that his father was keeping 'alive' in his barn.

Even darker is Carol's death. Driven to the point of despair by the rejection of the two people closest to her – Lori and Tyreese – she decides to commit suicide by offering herself to a walker tied up in the prison yard. The splash panel that depicts her death – as she smiles and whispers "Oh good… you do like me" as the zombie tears her throat out – remains one of the most chilling in any issue.

MAD, BAD WORLD

Carol's deteriorating mental state pushed her to the nastiest suicide imaginable. But she is not alone in wanting to end it all – the world of *The Walking Dead* is a harsh one and for those of an already fragile disposition it often becomes too much.

In the early days of the group's stay at the prison, Tyreese's daughter Julie and her boyfriend Chris make a suicide pact, agreeing to shoot each other at the same moment "to be together forever." But (almost inevitably) Chris shoots first and Julie dies in front of him, before rising again minutes later. In his rage, Tyreese strangles Chris, creating tension within the group and bringing the savage realities of death into the prison.

But as shocking as this moment is, it's nothing compared to the fate that befalls Hershel's twin daughters shortly after. If Carol, Julie and Chris's disturbed behaviour was ultimately directed towards themselves, the crazed mind of Thomas Richards leads him to kill others. The dual-decapitation of Susie and Rachel Greene is shocking and brutal, and marks a turning point for the group. Never again would they be as trusting of strangers as they were with the prison inmates; from that moment on, everyone – no matter if they're people or zombies – would be regarded as a potential threat.

As for Thomas, he is gunned down by Maggie, who rushes to save Patricia when she foolishly lets him out of his cell.

PULLING THE STRINGS

PULLING THE STRINGS

If Thomas was the first truly 'bad' character Rick's group encountered, he was hardly the last; plenty of gruesome death was to be unleashed by some truly despicable people over the next 100-plus issues. Ironically, the comic's biggest villains – most notably the Governor and Negan – largely rely on others to carry out their murderous deeds. But in both cases, their willingness to give the orders to kill makes it even more dramatic when they do get their hands dirty.

The Governor's prolonged public decapitation of Tyreese at the prison gates – shown in graphic detail over two full pages – makes it clear that the Woodbury leader will stop at nothing to get what he wants ("I don't think you realise how serious I am!"). His final bloody assault on the prison is littered with corpses on both sides.

DEAR, GOD... PLEASE.

JUST KILL ME.

TA TA

The sudden death of his son, Billy, is the final straw for Hershel, who has seen almost his entire family killed one after the other over a matter of a few months. Kneeling by his son's body, he tells Rick and the others to leave him as they flee the prison. "Oh please God, just kill me," he pleads to the Governor, who happily obliges.

And while it is an remorseful Lilly who pulls the trigger on Lori and baby Judith as they attempt to escape the prison, there is no question that the Governor is ultimately responsible for their demise. For those readers who might have become a bit desensitised by the sheer quantity of death over the previous 47 issues, this moment was a potent reminder of the shocking waste of human life, especially as they were the wife and child of the series' lead character.

If no other death has proven quite as upsetting as those of Judith and Lori, then *The Walking Dead*'s other big villain, Negan, is certainly giving the Governor a run for his money.

KIRKMAN AND ADLARD HAVE NEVER SHIED AWAY FROM SHOWING DEATH IN ALL ITS GRAPHIC, UPSETTING DETAIL, BUT GLENN'S DEMISE TOOK THE GORE TO ANOTHER LEVEL.

Issue 100 was always going to deliver something big, and the murder of Glenn was just that. Glenn was someone who had been a main character since the second issue, who had proven himself to be a much-loved, highly efficient member of the group. Not only that, but he is killed in front of his beloved Maggie, who is carrying their child.

Kirkman and artist Charlie Adlard have never shied away from showing death in all its graphic, upsetting detail, but Glenn's end – his head smashed to a pulp by Negan's barb-wire club, Lucille – took the gore to another level. The sight of Glenn's demolished cranium, post-beating, is not easily forgotten.

RED RIGHT HAND

Of course, it would be a mistake to think that all the killing in *The Walking Dead* is caused by zombies and villains while our heroes sit idly by. It would have been impossible for the likes of Rick, Michonne and Andrea to stay alive for so long without getting their hands dirty, and at times they have been as violent and unsparing as their foes.

Many of these deaths have been 'mercy' kills to stop already wounded team members from returning – think Lacey and Arnold Greene, shot by Hershel; or Andrea putting a bullet through her sister's head. But just as many were simply to protect the group; some completely justified, others less so.

It was Carl who stepped up and pulled the trigger on of the very first notable human victim, shooting Shane through the neck to protect his father.

Rick, too, has shown himself willing to go to any lengths to protect his family and friends – biting through the neck of a bandit threatening to rape and kill Carl or killing the sociopathic Pete Anderson in Alexandria ("We're better off without you. All of us."). But without doubt, the most controversial act of murderous preservation that Rick engages in is leading Michonne,

Abraham and Andrea to execute the cannibalistic Hunters, before burning their corpses.

For once, Kirkman and Adlard leave this massacre largely off-page. This is an act of killing that no one revels in, and the level of cold-blooded brutality shocks even the hardest members of the group. As Rick says, hours later: "I see every bloody bit. Every broken bone... every bashed in skull."

KIRKMAN UNDERSTANDS THAT A GORY DEATH IS ONE OF THE BIG DRAWS OF HIS STORIES, SO FREQUENTLY DISPATCHES CHARACTERS IN EXCITING, FUNNY AND THRILLING WAYS.

SHOCK WHILE THEY DROP

Nevertheless, Kirkman also understands that gory death is one of the big draws of his stories, so frequently dispatches characters in exciting, funny and thrilling ways.

Dwight, the Savior with a badly burnt face and deadly aim with a crossbow, is responsible for the dramatic death of one of the comic's best-loved characters, Abraham, shot mid-sentence with a bolt right through his eye.

The introduction of Michonne and her katana allowed for some spectacular killing, too – characters both minor and major end up tasting her steel, and it is no wonder that she quickly became a fan favourite. Her first appearance in issue 19 sees her beheading various walkers, but it wasn't long before human adversaries realized just how dangerous this mysterious sword-wielding lady could be. Just ask Woodbury cage fighter Eugene, or James Lee Steagal, one of the Governor's men whose head is cleaved spectacularly in half in issue 45. And, as well as the numerous Woodbury

soldiers, Hunters and Saviors that Michonne slices up along the way, her sword proves a highly effective method of ensuring the infected don't return – Tyreese, Gus, Scott, Denise and Morgan have all been recipients of this treatment.

The Walking Dead remains the most unpredictable comic book around, and when it comes to the messy, upsetting, dramatic business of death, there is clearly plenty more to come. If there's one lesson to learn from watching Kirkman and Adlard act as gleeful grim reapers for more than a decade, it is not to get too attached to any one character – the latest issue might well be their last.

TYREESE

There came a moment at the midway break of season three of AMC's *The Walking Dead* that had comic book fans punching the air with glee. When we encountered a new group of survivors, on the run and desperate, the identity of their burly leader was confirmed as he produced a familiar claw hammer. Tyreese had landed. We take a look over his time in the comic book.

WORDS: Sam Faulkner

SPOILER ALERT: IF YOU'RE NOT UP TO DATE, THIS FEATURE CONTAINS POTENTIAL SPOILER CONTENT FOR THE COMIC BOOK

FIRST ENCOUNTER

We first met comic book Tyreese after the dramatic events of Shane's death; as the Atlanta group moved away from the overrun city in issue seven, they were approached by a group of what they suspected were walkers. The figures were soon revealed to be a band of fellow survivors, led by the well-built Tyreese. Introduced in a large panel, with his bulky frame bundled in winter gear and his frightened followers behind him, it was clear from this first look that Tyreese would be a tower of strength and a fine addition to the group. And so began a storied relationship with the group and their leader, Rick.

"WHOA! WHOA! HOLD YOUR FIRE!"
FIRST WORDS SPOKEN, ISSUE SEVEN

MAN OF IRON

Tyreese is a physically imposing man, often either swathed in heavy layers of clothing, or with his powerful, muscular torso on display. There's always an outward sense of security when Tyreese is around, whatever the character's emotional state.

Usually a very squarely-drawn character, his strength is evident, standing taller and broader than most others. While his sturdy frame projects a calm demeanor, it is clear that Tyreese is not a guy to be trifled with – as we see when they reach the prison.

I TOLD YOU THIS WAS GOING TO SUCK.

HAMMERING IT HOME

In terms of contributing to the group, Tyreese is first and foremost a warrior. A former NFL journeyman, who was described as "not very good" by Falcons fan Michonne, the hulking Tyreese nevertheless has no problem taking down shambling walkers with meaty hits and brute force.

This was shown early on when he saved Rick from an undead assailant as the pair picked through the ruins of the gated community, Wiltshire Estates. With Rick in mortal danger and Dale unable to fire his weapon for fear of hitting the cop, Tyreese launches a huge tackle on the walker, before uttering the immortal line, "Let's paste these suckers!" It set the tone early on for how Tyreese would handle life post-zombie apocalypse, with his frequent gym sessions and deadliness with his signature hammer giving him the tools to become a true fan favorite.

For all his melee prowess, however, Tyreese never quite got the hang of firearms, with his uselessness with any kind of gun clearly shown as he struggles to hit the proverbial barn door. This has even been referenced in the TV series, as Tyreese, as played by Chad Coleman, tried and failed to get the hang of a rifle on the wall of Woodbury in season three – a fun nod to his comic book pedigree.

> "I GOT YOUR BACK, MAN. LET'S PASTE THESE SUCKERS!"

MORE BANG FOR HIS BUCK

Early on in the group's journey, Tyreese hooks up with Carol, giving the emotionally fragile survivor a broad shoulder to cry on. Tyreese's compassionate nature comes across in their relationship, as he supports Carol through some very dark times indeed.

Tyreese's actions cause conflict in the group on this occasion, proving just how difficult it is to be a boy scout in the walker-ravaged world of *The Walking Dead*. Tyreese's later comment that Carol "doesn't deserve my sorrow" shows just how flawed the formerly heroic character is.

"THIS HAMMER HAS WORKED JUST FINE FOR ME SO FAR!"

This makes it all the more heartbreaking when Michonne comes into the picture. She has plenty in common with Tyreese, and romance (or something like it in the gym!) is clearly on the cards early on.

It's at once upsetting and a sign of how flawed even a strong figure like Tyreese can be. It's hardly a clean break with Carol, leaving the vulnerable character in such an awful state that she attempts suicide.

I GUESS **NOW** WOULD NOT BE THE BEST TIME TO ADMIT TO YOU THAT I'M AFRAID OF THE **DARK.**

RICK. YOU'RE *BACK.*

WHAT *KEPT* YOU?

HIS GREATEST MOMENT

Putting together a comic book Tyreese highlights reel would entail a lot of swinging hammers and a mess of zombie brains splattering across the page.

After a number of high-impact walker kills in the early issues, including a heroic hit at the Wiltshire Estates (see previously), probably Tyreese's best moment came in issue 16. With Rick heading off from the prison to visit Shane's grave and take care of some gruesome unfinished business, Tyreese leads a group to try and retake the gym from the walker hordes. Swinging open the doors to face hundreds of the undead, the group take a handful out before being overwhelmed and forced to retreat. However, Tyreese, sick with rage following the death of his daughter, flies into the fray, heedless of the danger. The last we see of the mighty survivor is as a swarm of zombies descend upon him, with the rest of the group forced to abandon hope and flee the scene.

It appears to be a heroic end to the character, and when Rick returns to the prison and runs to the gym to confirm the fate of his friend, we get that fantastic panel of the bloodied Tyreese, sitting against a wall surrounded by dead walkers, saying, "Rick, you're back. What kept you?"

It's this scene alone that cements it as the character's best moment in the entire run.

"THE STUFF YOU'VE DONE TO SURVIVE, IT'S GIVEN YOU A BLOODLUST. YOU'RE STARTING TO ENJOY THE THINGS YOU DO."

HIS DARKEST HOUR

The earliest look at Tyreese's mettle being challenged was the tragic death of his teenage daughter Julie. She had been traveling with the group since the two parties met, along with boyfriend Chris, who we never quite trusted.

When Chris' plan to form a suicide pact with Julie gets dangerously real, Tyreese walks in on the pair in a cell at the prison, with Julie lying dead on the ground after Chris botched the attempt. Forced to watch his daughter die in his arms for the second time when Chris shoots her after she reanimates, Tyreese helps the cowardly young man on his way, leaping to the attack and throttling the life out of him.

"WHAT DID YOU DO? WHAT DID YOU DO TO MY LITTLE GIRL?"

This plunges the devoted father into an extremely dark place, having not only seen his beloved daughter die, but then taking a human life himself. Outwardly dealing with the tragedy after burning the bodies, Tyreese's emotional state is nevertheless irrevocably shaken by the events of his daughter's death.

Later, after Rick confronts Tyreese following the switch of his affections from Carol to Michonne, the friends are drawn into a physical altercation that takes a huge toll on the pair, both physically and emotionally. As they trade blows, their strong alliance appears to be over, and Rick is left beaten and broken by the encounter. The exchange forces members of the group to question Rick's leadership, which in turn leads to one of the most iconic moments of the comic book run – Rick's "We *are* the walking dead" speech. The pair eventually patch up their differences, but this was unquestionably a rough time for all involved.

"WE CAN'T JUST IGNORE THE RULES, RICK. WE'VE GOT TO RETAIN OUR HUMANITY."

TYREESE FACT FILE
NAME: Tyreese
PLAYED BY IN TV SERIES: Chad Coleman
AGE: Late 30s-early 40s (est.)
JOB: Former pro-football player; security
FAMILY: Daughter (Julie – deceased [unique to the comic book]); sister (Sasha – alive [unique to the TV series])
RELATIONSHIPS POST-APOCALYPSE: Carol, Michonne
LIKES: His daughter, Rick, working out, the Atlanta Falcons, BJs, his claw hammer
DISLIKES: Chris, Chris, Chris. Chris! CHRIS! (And the Governor, of course…)
FIRST APPEARANCE: Issue seven (comic); season three, episode eight, 'Made To Suffer' (TV)
CURRENT STATUS: Deceased

"DON'T LET HIM IN! DON'T…" FINAL WORDS SPOKEN, ISSUE 46

TIME TO DIE

Of course, Tyreese's lowest moment in the comic book came in issue 46, with his death at the hands of the Governor. After setting off on an ill-fated rescue mission to Woodbury with Michonne to try to kill the despotic leader, the pair are separated and Tyreese captured. The Governor returns to the prison with Tyreese bound in the back of his truck, but his attempt to use Tyreese as a bargaining chip to gain entry to the prison fails. Rick's hard choice to call his enemy's bluff proves to be the end of Tyreese. The Governor doesn't bluff.

Using Michonne's own katana, he cruelly kills Tyreese, hacking at the defenseless prisoner's neck until, with one disdainful boot, the Governor kicks his head clean off his shoulders. It was an inglorious end to such a popular character. It's times like these that reveal just how cold and heartless Robert Kirkman can be as a writer when he needs harsh actions to serve his story.

That said, at least we get to meet Tyreese again in the TV show.

FAN DEVOTION

As an all-action fighter and a pillar of strength in the survivor community, it's easy to see why and how Tyreese became such a popular figure.

From the first time we met him, it was clear that this was a strong man who would protect those under his care. He had natural leadership abilities and was clear-headed and pragmatic, but was, on the whole, happy to play defensive linesman to Rick's quarterback. The two

rarely clashed, apart from one devastating bout, and the big man's devotion as a father was clear for all to see – eventually leading to his emotional vulnerability.

Over the course of Tyreese's run in the comic books, we took a real journey with the character – going through heartbreak, happiness, violence, and desperation. Despite such a stoic outward appearance and no-nonsense attitude to dealing with problems, he always had an appealing humanity about him, showing his flaws

and sometimes struggling to keep his emotions in check.

Tyreese's death was an incredibly sad moment, especially in such a nasty fashion, and caused much outrage and controversy among the fans – just check out the comics' Letter Hacks pages around issue 49 if you don't believe us! He had been a tough and dependable mainstay of the group since issue seven and had built up a strong fan base of followers.

MAKING A SPLASH

One of the highlights of Charlie Adlard's *The Walking Dead* artwork is his tremendous 'splash panels' (full page or double page illustrations). They are used minimally, but when he does do them, they are always memorable. *TWDM* looks at one of his most impactful splashes featured in the comic. **WORDS: Dan Auty**

HOW DID WE GET HERE?

This splash panel appears in issue 59. Rick, Carl and Abraham are on the road, trying to find somewhere safe for the group to stay. They have just left Rick's old hometown, having found Morgan, and are on their way back. As morning comes and they head down a hill, they are confronted by a huge swarm of walkers, lumbering hungrily towards them.

WHAT'S THE SCENE?

This incredibly dramatic image shows the steep incline of the hill, as the truck speeds down it. The road stretches before them, eventually winding out of sight. Abraham is stationed in the back, gun readied to blast the oncoming zombies who are spread out far into the distance.

ALL ABOUT THE NUMBERS

The splash itself is free from words and sound effects, instead letting Charlie Adlard's illustration do all the talking. Its biggest strength is that it defies horror convention – the scene is in broad daylight and in the biggest 'setting' possible, the outside world. It works so well because it presents walkers at their most dangerous – in overwhelming numbers. The angle of the truck adds to the tension: its wheels skidding, the vehicle spins awkwardly towards the mass of zombies, while the road winds away into the distance, highlighting just how unprepared the unlucky quartet were for such a sight.

WIDE OPEN SPACES

This image is a perfect demonstration of the sudden dramatic power of a splash. However, it would not have nearly the same impact without the last panel on the previous page, a close-up of Rick's face as he exclaims "Oh my God!" To turn over from a tight close-up of someone's face to a huge, widescreen vista makes for thrilling reading. •

THE SECRET DIARY OF A WALKER

It's not easy being a zombie in *The Walking Dead* world, as our week in the life/death of an undead walker shows. Diary entries transcribed by Dan Auty…

Monday

Another week in what feels like the longest summer vacation ever for my kids. I swear they've been off for months now, with no sign of going back to school. It doesn't help that they ate their mom weeks ago…

Tuesday

The young couple from next door, Steven and Fran, popped round. They suggested I take the kids up to this adventure park they've heard about. It's called The Kingdom – sounds like it might have some animals to look at. Steven and Fran were planning on going there anyway, so we'll just tag along. They said it was OK.

Wednesday

We've had to delay our fun day out – Steven woke up this morning with half his face stuck to his pillow. At least he matches Fran – she's been missing a jaw for about three weeks now. And I thought young people cared about their appearance…

Thursday

The kids were so excited about tomorrow's trip to The Kingdom that they could barely sleep last night. I caught them both having a midnight feast – they'd taken the last pot of guts from the fridge. I'd normally be angry but they looked so sweet with intestinal gore smeared around their mouths that I just had to forgive them.

Friday

Our trip to The Kingdom didn't go quite as well as we'd hoped…

First of all, it's not a wildlife park at all – the place is swarming with normos. Which would be fine if they were in cages, but this lot were running around with guns and making a helluva noise. Poor old Steve ended up getting a bullet right through what remained of his face. We managed to get out of there just in time. We're staying at home next summer! •

LIFE AMONG THEM

With AMC's adaptation of *The Walking Dead* reaching the Alexandria storyline from the comic, *TWDM* decided it was time to take stock of this key moment on the page. In 'Life Among Them,' Rick and his team find fitting back into a surburban lifestyle more difficult than they could possibly imagine.

WORDS: Stuart Barr

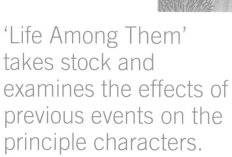

T he 'Fear The Hunters' storyline (volume 11) demonstrated how dark a path decent people could walk. Dale's death and the violent and merciless retribution meted out to his cannibalistic killers by Rick Grimes and his group has left a stain on their souls. Volume 11 closed with Rick discovering his son Carl had taken the life of psychotic child Ben. These events compounded by increasing problems in sourcing food has left the survivors physically and psychologically drained.

Volume 12: *Life Among Them* downshifts gears and slows the pace. It is a transitional story leading towards a shift from flight to fight. Featuring only sporadic action (this is the second volume

> 'Life Among Them' takes stock and examines the effects of previous events on the principle characters.

to feature no fatalities among the living), 'Life Among Them' is interested in taking stock and examining the effects of the previous events on the principle characters. The survivors have lost so much, their homes at the prison and the Greene family farm, many friends and loved ones, and possibly their humanity in the desperate and dangerous journey to Washington.

The volume begins with Rick cresting a hilltop and observing a town infested with walkers. Although a lack of food has become an increasingly serious issue, the town is too overrun and the group too weak to search it safely. In a clear attempt to move away from the terrible revelation over Ben's death, Rick and Carl reminisce about comfort food from before the fall of civilization. "Remember pizza?"

If the group continue to stick to rural areas less infested by the dead they are safer from physical harm, but the food supplies found in abandoned dwellings are dwindling. Homes and stores have now been ransacked many times over. Suburban and urban areas were more populated before the outbreak, and are now more infested by walkers. Yet this very threat means food supplies are less plundered. Ever watched a nature documentary where thirst forces gazelles to creep towards a croc-infested water hole? The group is not starving yet (Carl is still able to turn his nose up at oatmeal), but facing this brutal dilemma is not far away.

A glimmer of hope lies in Washington and the promise of a cure offered by Dr Eugene Porter. This is snatched away when it is revealed that Eugene has lied about both the cure and his need to

Aaron offers a message of hope, claiming to be an emissary and scout for a nearby safe haven.

get to Washington. There is no research facility, he is just an overweight high school science teacher who concocted a tall tale so stronger people would protect him. Having lost lives keeping him safe, Sgt Abraham Ford reacts particularly badly, beating Eugene to the ground (although not as severely as in the television version, where Eugene is left comatose).

However, before the implications of Eugene's lie can really register, a stranger arrives on the scene: Aaron approaches the group, palms out and unarmed. Rick's immediate reaction is to knock him out and tie him up. While this is understandable given past history, even Abraham is taken aback by Rick's ferocity.

In the interrogation that follows, Aaron offers a message of hope, claiming to be an emissary and scout for a nearby safe haven. The outpost has food

and secure walls to keep out the undead, as well as medicine, doctors, even a surgeon. What they lack is enough people to maintain their security and scout for necessary supplies. Aaron has been observing Rick's group for days, sizing them up as potential new community members. After his experiences with the Governor, Rick is naturally suspicious. After all, as he notes, the Governor was "all smiles" when they first met him, and Woodbury also had a physician.

Rick's misgivings are overruled by the group. It is Michonne who

galvanizes support to join Aaron's community. "If we don't do this – if we let this pass us by – what are we doing here?" Even if the rest of the group voted to walk on, Michonne is adamant that she is taking up Aaron's offer.

The next day the group meet Aaron's partner, Eric, and discover they used a parabolic microphone to listen to them. Eric and Aaron are also lovers. The first openly gay relationship in *The Walking Dead* is presented in a matter of fact way, and unequivocally accepted without comment by the survivors. Like racism, sexism and other prejudices, there really is no place for homophobia in *The Walking Dead* – the

a significant amount of trust-building still to be done to win Rick over.

The tense journey of the convoy is interrupted when a distant flare signals that supply runners from Aaron's settlement are in distress. This allows Rick and Abraham to bloodily demonstrate their prowess at zombie slaughter before a rescue

party arrives. Abraham's approach to triage assessment does little to endear Aaron's potential new recruits to the other scouts. The episode also gives a brief glimpse of how hostile central Washington has become for those with blood pumping in their veins. Escaping the horde along East Capital Street in the shadow of the city's landmarks, Rick grimly chuckles, "Always wanted to come here."

The group arrives at the walls of the settlement and discover its name, the Alexandria Safe-Zone. It is the idyll promised by Aaron. While outside the walls lies walker-ravaged Washington, inside this gated community children play in its streets. On seeing the carefree, playful children, Rick remarks that was "not something I thought I'd ever see again."

> Like racism, sexism and other prejudices, there really is no place for homophobia in *The Walking Dead*.

IN A NUTSHELL

TITLE: Life Among Them
FEATURED ISSUES: 67-72
COLLECTION: Volume 12
SYNOPSIS: Following their encounter with the cannibalistic Hunters, Rick's group meets Aaron, a herald from a nearby survivor community who invites Rick and the others to join them. When they reach the Alexandria Safe-Zone, Rick's group are interviewed by its leader, Douglas Monroe, who gives them jobs in the community that suit their varied skills. Rick, for instance, is given the role of the community's resident cop. Rick and the rest initially struggle to leave their survivor mentality behind and conflict between the two groups arise. Although the Alexandrians have been nothing but welcoming, Rick plans a coup.

TIDBITS:
- This is the second volume to feature no deaths of living characters. Quite a few zombies still get it though.

- 'Life Among Them' features the comic's first openly gay couple, Aaron and Eric.

- Rick shaves his beard off when he reaches Alexandria. It's the first time we've seen him without at least a bit of stubble on his chin since the very first page of issue one.

- The comic doesn't use flashback much as a narrative device, setting the story mostly in the present. However, when Michonne hangs up her sword, we see her memories pour forth, including torturing the Governor, fighting in the Woodbury gladiatorial ring, the death of Tyreese and saving Carl in the car (from volume nine). One flashback memory we had previously never seen before shows Michonne cutting off the arms of her boyfriend and his best friend, Mike and Terry. The story is elaborated on in the Michonne Special released in March 2012, almost two years after this issue (#72) was published.

people living in its nightmarish world, where the undead munch on the living, have far more important things to deal with. This is not to say that writer Robert Kirkman shies away from touching on such hot topics on occasion, but it's clear that salvation from the very real threat of the zombies lies in trusting other people, whatever their background or sexuality.

Trust is a big issue for Rick, and he is more than a little concerned that Aaron had not mentioned working with a partner. Clearly for Aaron, there's

> The extreme stress and trauma of living in this wrecked world has affected all the long-running characters.

The discussion of pizza at the opening of the volume neatly foreshadows a theme for this volume: comfort.

THAT CREEPY OLD BASTARD JUST HIT ON ME.

companion. As she hangs it above the mantel place of her new home, she addresses it with finality: "I'm through with you." It's a symbolic narrative move: while Rick arrives at Alexandria weighed down by suspicion and doubt, Michonne chooses to leave all that behind and accept a new reality.

While Alexandria represents new hope for the members of Rick's group, it's not all roses. A particularly 'odd' note occurs during Douglas' interview of Andrea, where he suddenly asks her if she is single. It's a startling question, for both reader and Andrea, which he brushes off as a way of helping him to know relationship statuses when assigning quarters to new arrivals. Later, however, the question is put into more telling context when he really puts the moves on Andrea, revealing he has an 'open marriage.'

On this occasion, he's chosen the wrong person: Andrea is still deeply traumatized by the recent death of her lover, Dale, and both of her adopted charges, Ben and Billy. Her rejection of Douglas is accepted without complaint, but it still strikes a curious note. Douglas' behavior could be seen as an exploitation of his status that sits at odds with the apparent equality of the Safe-Zone (this is a storyline notably absent in the TV retelling, where Deanna is happily married).

The leader of the Alexandria Safe-Zone is a former state senator, Douglas Monroe (Deanna Monroe in the TV show), who interviews Rick and his group and assigns them roles in the community. As a sheriff in his pre-apocalypse life, Rick is understandably appointed Alexandria's new constable. Weapons are not allowed to be carried or kept within the

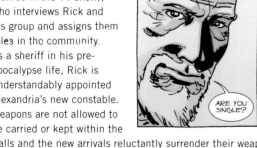

ARE YOU SINGLE?

EXCUSE ME?

walls and the new arrivals reluctantly surrender their weapons for safekeeping to Alexandria's armory. Only Michonne is permitted to keep her sword, on the proviso that she mounts it on her new home's wall. In a telling move, the katana becomes an ornament, a memento of life outside the walls, rather than a weapon.

The Walking Dead has wrestled before with mental health issues. The extreme stress and trauma of living in this wrecked world has affected all the long-running characters. Rick talked to his dead wife on a plastic telephone, and Michonne's katana is more than just a sword to her, it has been her most constant

At a party thrown in honor of the new arrivals, it becomes clear that moving on is hard for more of the group than just Andrea and Rick. Suddenly switching from living on your wits in a constant fight for survival to an environment where people worry about hors d'oeuvres is difficult, even for Michonne. Other members of the group also react poorly: Carl flies into a rage when his beloved Stetson is assumed to be a cowboy outfit, and Glenn becomes a drunken fool after imbibing too much alcohol, deeply embarrassing his wife. Morgan and Michonne, two people who have been to the edge of madness and just about come back, seek

While Rick undeniably sees the community's value and wishes it to become his home, he also sees it as a prize too good for the sheep.

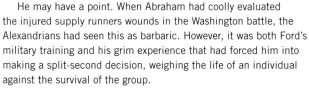

a little solace in each other's arms.

The discussion of pizza at the opening of the volume neatly foreshadows a major theme for this volume: comfort. The Alexandria Safe-Zone represents the closest return to a semblance of pre-fall civilization since Woodbury, but where the Governor's community was a thinly disguised fascistic state, Alexandria is built on communal (almost communist) principles. The comforts of a lost world are powerful attractions, and all the adults are drawn to it. Even Rick quickly sees the Alexandria Safe-Zone as a potential home. Perhaps because he is someone who has entered adolescence in the world of the undead, it is Carl who rejects the community the most, telling his father it is "pretend."

He may have a point. When Abraham had coolly evaluated the injured supply runners wounds in the Washington battle, the Alexandrians had seen this as barbaric. However, it was both Ford's military training and his grim experience that had forced him into making a split-second decision, weighing the life of an individual against the survival of the group.

Monroe and Aaron may recognize that this is a strength they need. The children may play in the streets here, the adults may have cold beer in the ice-box and hot running water. But at what price does this innocence and safety come? How prepared are the Alexandrians for the world outside those walls?

Perhaps it's because of this that Rick does not integrate immediately into Monroe's happy commune. While he undeniably sees the community's value and wishes it to become his home, he also sees it as a prize too good for the sheep. As it turns out, Glenn's drunkenness is merely a ruse used as a cover for intelligence gathering. The group have been quietly scoping out Alexandria, finding the community's weak spots and plotting a coup. Douglas Monroe sees Rick's group as useful additions to his community, but perhaps it is a more realistic outcome that it is the Alexandrians who will be forced to join Rick's group.

Is Rick the shepherd or the wolf? The story's title, 'Life Among Them,' is perhaps the telling answer. •

ZOMBIE KILL OF THE WEEK

Although it's usually best to run away from the undead, sometimes there's no option but to be a little more aggressive. Splatter fan Dan Auty draws a chalk outline round some of the comic's best kills…

WHO…
Andrea. One of the few remaining original survivors, Andrea reminds us just how handy she is with some cold steel in her hand.

WHERE…
This juicy kill takes place on the edge of the Alexandria Safe Zone. Andrea is teaching a small group of survivors, including Maggie, Olivia and Aaron, a spot of target practice. Their tuition is interrupted by the arrival of a horde of shambling walkers looking for some lunch. Andrea tells her pupils to engage in some 'live' practice – as the zombies approach, the group

let fly with their bullets. Some hit the target, most don't. At that point, our gun-toting heroine takes over.

HOW…
After dispatching most of the zombies at a distance, Andrea calmly explains to the group that the closer the roamer is, the better the chance of killing it with a single shot, saving vital bullets. She allows the final slavering walker to lurch right up to her, before raising her weapon to its rotting forehead and blowing its brains all over the page.

WITH…
A handgun. It's nothing fancy, but in

the right hands, it's brutally effective when it comes to dropping walkers.

THE AFTERMATH
Rick, watching from the side, tells the group what they had already figured out: "That, ladies and gentlemen, is why Andrea is heading up our gun training." Ever modest, she replies: "Point and shoot – it's not hard." But they both know that Andrea's role in keeping the group safe is a vital one.

THE SECRET DIARY OF A WALKER

It's not easy being a zombie in *The Walking Dead* world, as our week in the life/death of an undead walker shows. Diary entries transcribed by Dan Auty…

MONDAY
Dear Diary…
Woke up with a terrible hangover, facedown in a swamp. Once I'd managed to work out where I was, I noticed two things. First, I'd lost an arm. Second – and more alarmingly – I was wearing the most revolting shirt. I know, 'zombie chic' is so last year, but there's no excuse for such sartorial aberration. This week's priorities: 1) Find lunch; 2) Update wardrobe.

TUESDAY
Man, this swamp is dull. Met a couple of guys – we all agreed that swampy woodland probably isn't the best place to find fresh brains. One of them has heard of a farm nearby, so we're heading that way now.

WEDNESDAY
More swamp. No brains. What I'd give for a juicy liver right now. Have abandoned my new friends, too – I know I've looked better, but those guys were embarrassing. OK, you might not have a jaw but at least make an effort.

THURSDAY
Much better day. Finally made it out of the swamp and have spotted the farm. The 'normos' look like a nice bunch: men, women, kids and some old dude who keeps saying zombies are his friends. Looking forward to eating, er, I mean meeting him tomorrow.

FRIDAY
Day started well enough. I strolled over to the farm – the old guy didn't even want to shoot me, which makes a nice change.

But then, annoyingly, the barn was full of other zombies. Before you could say "Humngg!", they're getting in my way, grabbing all the juicy trimmings. I know my kind have an image problem, but a few manners wouldn't go amiss.

Oh well, you die, you learn, you die again…

MEET THE NEW RECRUITS

Abraham, Rosita and Eugene may be new additions to AMC's *The Walking Dead*, but they have been around in the comic since issue 53. With the trio all still alive in the TV series, *TWDM* thought it a good idea to check out their comic book credentials in preparation for the next season. So here's everything you need to know about Sgt Ford, Ms Espinosa and Dr Porter. But be warned: potential spoilers ahead.

WORDS: Stuart Barr

Followers of AMC's *The Walking Dead* are just getting to know the characters of Sergeant Abraham Ford, Rosita Espinosa and Eugene Porter, but readers of the comic will be very familiar with them. As played in their TV incarnations by Michael Cudlitz, Christian Serratos and Josh McDermitt respectively, the TV versions of the characters look remarkably similar to their comic book templates.

The trio entered the saga in the period following the fall of the prison (*Volume 9: Here We Remain*, issue 53), arriving at the Greene family farm after the demoralized survivors of the bloodbath are regrouping. At a particularly dark time for Rick and the other survivors, these new arrivals ignited new hope and spurred the group to leave the farm and head to Washington DC.

SGT ABRAHAM FORD

"You don't rip a man apart… hold his insides in your hand… you can't go back to being dear old dad after that." Issue 57

BACKGROUND

A distinctive figure, usually portrayed in a vest and military fatigues and always sporting his trademark handlebar moustache, Abraham was a US Army sergeant and sports coach before the zombie plague. In the early stages of the crisis, he lost his ex-wife, eight-year-old son and six-year-old daughter in horrific circumstances. As society crumbled, Abraham gathered his family together and joined a band of survivors – people he knew and trusted. However, while out on a supply mission, some of the men raped his wife and daughter and forced his son to watch. Upon his return, Abraham killed those responsible with his bare hands, but his unshackled rage terrified his family and they fled. Abraham tracked them down, only to find they had been consumed by walkers. The experience has left him ridden with guilt.

"WE COULD SIT AROUND AND COMPARE THE HORRORS WE'VE ALL FACED BUT I DON'T FEEL LIKE WE'RE CLOSE ENOUGH FOR ME TO CRY IN FRONT OF YOU JUST YET."
ABRAHAM, ISSUE 54

STRENGTHS

Abraham's main attributes lie in his military skill and leadership qualities. As part of the Alexandria Safe-Zone

community, Abraham led a work crew performing dangerous but necessary work repairing the crumbling walls around the compound. He's practical, resourceful, strong and an experienced warrior.

"I'M NOTICING A DISTURBING TREND. YOU GUYS POINT A GUN AT ANYONE WHO DISAGREES WITH YOU. WISH I'D NOTICED SOONER."
ABRAHAM TO RICK, ISSUE 56

WEAKNESSES

Abraham's greatest weakness is a dangerous temper. He often butted heads with Rick, even attempting to take over leadership of the group on one occasion – he almost allowed Rick to die at the hands of a walker, stepping in to save him only at the last moment. The initial distrust and mutual antagonism between these two alpha males eventually evolved into respect, but it was a slow and painful process. The pivotal moment came when Abraham opened up to Rick while on the road and told him the story of his family's annihilation.

Abe's let his quick temper get him into many tricky situations, usually because he has a tendency to blurt out his thoughts before thinking about what he's saying. Ford's treatment of Rosita has been questionable at times. Arriving as a couple, their relationship hit complications when Abraham cheated on her with Holly, a resident of Alexandria. In a moment of extreme emotional cruelty, Abraham told Rosita he'd never loved her, and was only with her out of pity as she felt like the last woman on Earth. This may have been an act of self-deception, with Abraham psychologically compelled to destroy his own happiness, but this darkness within may have been the reason behind his divorce pre-apocalypse.

CURRENT WHEREABOUTS

Abraham's death was one of the most shockingly 'casual' in *The Walking Dead*, cut down by a sniper's crossbow bolt. An ignoble end for a born warrior, but an example of the arbitrary nature of life and death in *The Walking Dead*.

"CAREFUL NOW. YOUR INSECURITY IS SHOWING... YOU DON'T WANT THESE PEOPLE TO START SEEING THROUGH THAT HEADSTRONG MACHO PERSONALITY LIKE I DO."
ROSITA TO ABRAHAM, ISSUE 64

ROSITA ESPINOSA

"I loved him, but he loved you. I'm sorry for your loss." Issue 99

BACKGROUND
Very little is known about Rosita's life before the outbreak, it is presumed that she is from the Houston area, but even that detail is sketchy.

STRENGTHS
Rosita has a rare emotional maturity and empathy towards others. Without her calming influence it is extremely doubtful that Abraham would have stayed among Rick's group for long given his mood

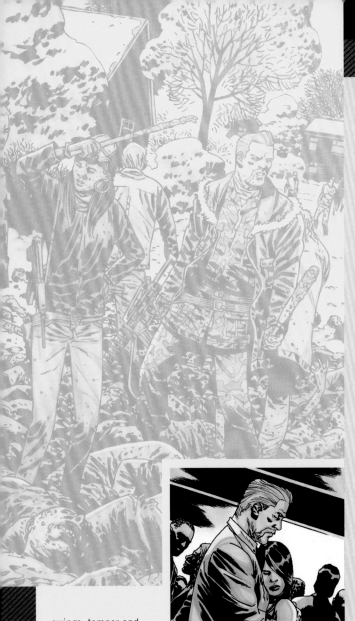

swings, temper and
his initial antagonism
with Rick. At the same
time, she was no meek
girlfriend; she appeared to understand Abraham, was aware
of his potential for violence, and would stand up to him and
criticize his behavior when she felt it necessary. Rosita clearly
loved and cared for Abraham, but when their relationship
ended, she moved on to a 'relationship' with Eugene.

Rosita is able to integrate into new groups, and is the sort
of person who can get along with others and handle difficult
personalities. She carries her own pistols and appears capable
with them: whether she came by these combat skills herself or
learnt them from Abraham is unknown. During the Alexandria
Safe-Zone breach incident, she was invaluable in the desperate
defense against an invasion of walkers.

WEAKNESSES

Rosita has been very much a supporting character in the comic,
so while it is hard to single out any particular character flaws,
it could perhaps be said that she is content to be the strong
woman in the background.

EUGENE PORTER

"I believe your beliefs are absurd." Issue 63

BACKGROUND

So there's the truth and there's the fiction. The truth is 'Doctor'
Eugene Porter is a former high-school science teacher. Coming
to the grim realization that he was not best placed to survive
the apocalypse – he is not a fit man, and squeamish over the
grim necessities of survival after the outbreak – he concocted an
elaborate ruse to appear invaluable to others and found strong
relationships with those who could protect him. Eugene claimed
to be a US Government scientist with a link to a surviving research
facility and with knowledge of important information that could lead
to a vaccine. He saw in Abraham a strong protector and in return
gave Ford a reason to live after the death of his family. Although his
lie led his companion frequently into harm's way, it is just as true to
say that on an important level Porter indirectly saved his life.

> "I KNOW YOU'VE BEEN LONELY THESE LAST FEW
> WEEKS. I COULD MAKE YOU HAPPY. I KNOW
> WHAT YOU LIKE. IF YOU WOULD ONLY LET ME
> TRY." EUGENE TO ROSITA, ISSUE 93

STRENGTHS

His wits. Eugene recognized his own physical shortcomings,
which make survival challenging for him, and used his
intelligence to craft a story that was partially plausible. The
desire of others to believe him did most of the heavy lifting,

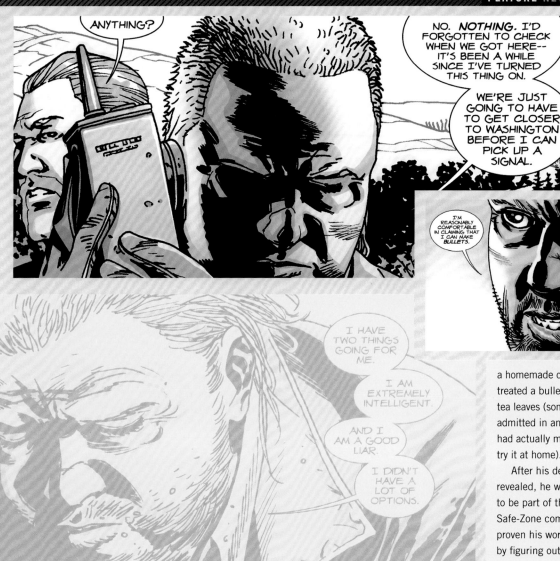

ANYTHING?

NO. **NOTHING.** I'D FORGOTTEN TO CHECK WHEN WE GOT HERE-- IT'S BEEN A WHILE SINCE I'VE TURNED THIS THING ON.

WE'RE JUST GOING TO HAVE TO GET CLOSER TO WASHINGTON BEFORE I CAN PICK UP A SIGNAL.

I'M REASONABLY COMFORTABLE IN CLAIMING THAT I CAN MAKE BULLETS.

I HAVE TWO THINGS GOING FOR ME.

I AM EXTREMELY INTELLIGENT.

AND I AM A GOOD LIAR.

I DIDN'T HAVE A LOT OF OPTIONS.

a homemade compass; he treated a bullet wound with tea leaves (something Kirkman admitted in an interview he had actually made up, so don't try it at home).

After his deception was revealed, he was still allowed to be part of the Alexandria Safe-Zone community. He has proven his worth subsequently by figuring out a way to make precious ammunition.

WEAKNESSES

We have to mention the hair. One of the greatest acts of suspension of disbelief in *The Walking Dead* is that we are expected to believe anyone would imagine someone with Eugene's hideous mullet is a genius. When confronted about his haircut, he again showed his razor sharp wits by claiming he was disguising himself as a doofus.

Eugene is overweight and unfit, can't shoot worth a damn, and frankly is of little practical use in combat. He also has an unusual affliction for someone who's based his relationships on a lie (albeit one designed to keep him alive): he has humanist values. When the Saviors threaten the Washington area communities, he initially refused to make ammunition, as it would be used against live humans rather than walkers. •

I DON'T THINK YOU QUITE UNDERSTAND THE SITUATION.

"I'M ONE OF 10 PEOPLE WHO WERE WORKING ON A PROJECT TO MAP THE HUMAN GENOME WHEN THE PLAGUE HIT... I KNOW EXACTLY WHAT CAUSED THE DEAD TO START WALKING, STRANGER." EUGENE, ISSUE 53

and then he used his high-school science knowledge to 'amaze' his companions enough to create the impression he was a genius. It was a clever confidence trick – Eugene must have been a great teacher.

His knowledge of science does have practical uses. He cured Abraham of headaches by manipulating pressure points; he created

TOP 5

We pick five of our *Walking Dead* favorites, from characters and moments to lines of dialogue, weapons, deaths and more.
WORDS: Russell Cook

SGT ABRAHAM QUOTES

5. "I want her to be happy without me. Like I am without her. I just want things to be right. Do you understand?"

In issue 98, as an arrow embeds itself into his eye socket, Abraham tells his friend Eugene that he hopes his ex, Rosita, will find romantic happiness after their break-up. This display of humanity, right in the throes of death, shows that, despite the emotional journey endured while spending each day hunted by disease-ridden dead folk, a desire for human connection is always omnipresent, regardless of circumstance. Despite whatever the world, and, in particular, *The Walking Dead* world throws at you, relationships with people are everything.

4. "I can't get over how easy it was. How much it didn't upset me. I can't get over how much I've changed. How much my family would hate what I've become."

While Abraham is a man of duty, seemingly putting the mission above all else, he was a family man once. In issue 58, he admits to Rick that he killed six people with his bare hands for raping his wife and daughter, before going on to add he's killed many more. This quote reveals how far across the lines of morality he is willing to go. Like many of Abe's best lines, it's layered with underlying pathos. His inner conflict and the ongoing dilemma about what's now right or wrong are issues that affect all the survivors.

3. "This isn't about emotions! It's about goddamn common sense!"

Abraham is as dry, matter-of-fact and emotionless as ever in issue 56 when he tells the group that they need to shoot Maggie before she reanimates, while a distraught Glenn believes she will survive, despite having found her not breathing and swinging from a tree with a rope around her neck. Thankfully, Abe was wrong, and the whole affair did leave him looking pretty bad. However, it did prove he's not afraid to make the difficult decisions.

2. "Yeah. Let's fuck this dog."

Abraham has quite the silver tongue, doesn't he? Man, woman, child, his words are not for mincing. Heading out to make a supply run in issue 88, he delivers this eloquent line. Now, bearing in mind, Abe is a military man, prettying up a subject just isn't his forte. As a result, he has some pretty colorful chat – mostly the kind you'd hear on the battlefield during a tour of Afghanistan. And we love it!

1. "There may be some group of dick faces out there... wanting to pick us off one by one. That's no reason to panic."

These words, from issue 64, highlight Abe's attitude towards life after the apocalypse – he lives each day like it's a mission and his confidence and appearance of strength, along with his unashamed personality, help give the group an added sense of purpose. His military experience and a childlike competition shine through here, summing up his character in a nutshell.

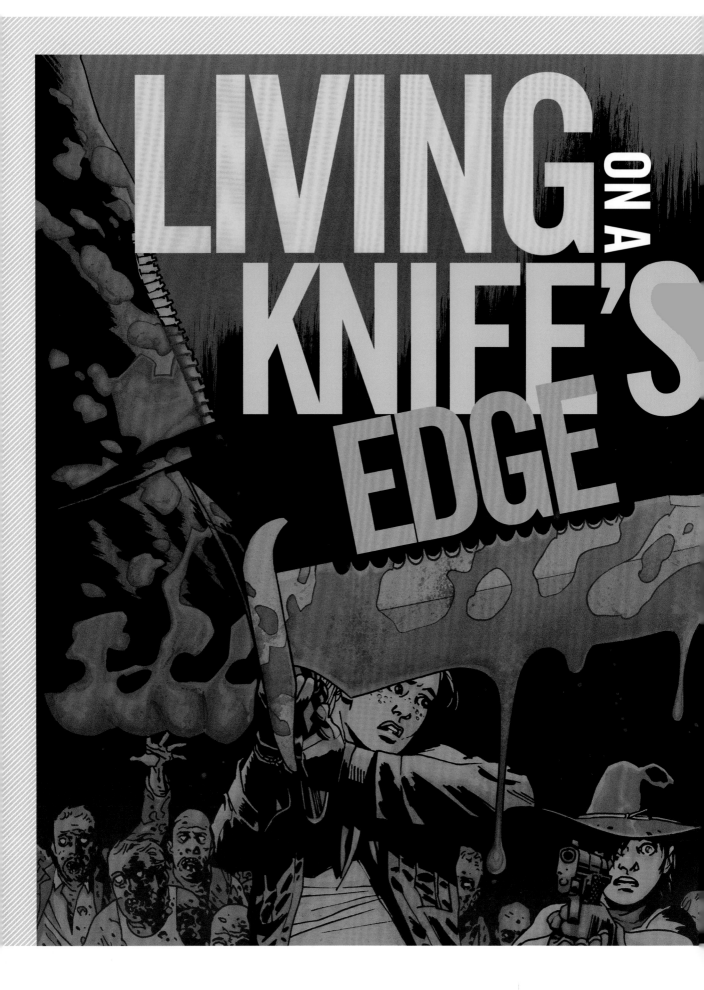

What's it take to survive in *The Walking Dead*? Guts? Skills? Luck? A warrior instinct? *TWDM* takes a look at why the longest survivors of the comic book series have the right stuff in a wrong world, and picks out those with a lasting legacy (to date!). WORDS: Rich Matthews

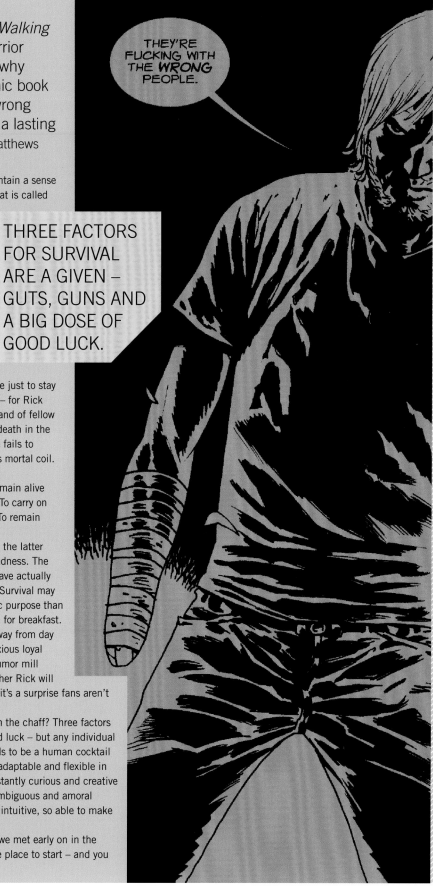

"Even in times of trauma, we try to maintain a sense of normality until we no longer can. That is called surviving. But those of us who have made it through hell and are still standing? We bear a different name: warriors." – Lori Goodwin, Iraq War veteran

The last word that springs to mind when talking about *The Walking Dead* is "normal." Scary, yes. Apocalyptic, certainly. Tough, definitely. But never normal. However, the characters of Robert Kirkman's comic book opus have lived through well over a hundred issues in their zombie-ravaged world, where humanity's more primal nature has had to come to the fore just to stay alive. To co-opt a buzz-term from recent years – for Rick Grimes, his family and the eccentric rag-tag band of fellow survivors that they encounter, literally staring death in the face has become the new norm. And if anyone fails to adjust, they inevitably end up shuffling off this mortal coil. Then shuffle until they rot.

The dictionary defines 'survive' as: 1) To remain alive or in existence; to live longer than, outlive; 2) To carry on despite hardships or trauma, to persevere; 3) To remain functional or usable.

The first two definitions are very literal, but the latter really fits the notion of finding normality in madness. The irony is that the events of *The Walking Dead* have actually brought our species nearer to our true nature. Survival may well just be a matter of accepting a more basic purpose than updating our statuses or tweeting what we had for breakfast. Having said that, only Rick has lasted all the way from day one – and the longer he survives, the more anxious loyal readers become about his eventual fate (the rumor mill has been revolving so fast recently about whether Rick will survive or not in both the comic and TV show, it's a surprise fans aren't starting to feel dizzy).

So, what is it that separates the wheat from the chaff? Three factors are a given – guts, guns and a big dose of good luck – but any individual who makes it through catastrophic events tends to be a human cocktail of certain key traits. They are resilient; highly adaptable and flexible in their thinking; pragmatic in their outlook; constantly curious and creative when confronted with obstacles; unfazed by ambiguous and amoral events; fiercely independent; and perceptively intuitive, so able to make insightful choices in a split second.

So, when looking at the half-dozen people we met early on in the saga who still possess a pulse, there's only one place to start – and you gotta respect the law...

> ## THREE FACTORS FOR SURVIVAL ARE A GIVEN – GUTS, GUNS AND A BIG DOSE OF GOOD LUCK.

> THEY'RE FUCKING WITH THE *WRONG* PEOPLE.

RICK GRIMES

RICK'S PERFECTLY SUITED TO A MORE BASIC, TOUGHER EXISTENCE. HE'S A MAN OF A BYGONE ERA, BROUGHT BACK INTO SHARP RELEVANCE.

FIRST APPEARANCE: ISSUE ONE

You've got to have something worth living for, and for Rick it's his son, Carl. From the moment he woke up from his coma, Rick had a mission, a purpose – find his family and protect them. The objects of his affections beyond Carl may have changed – wife and mother Lori didn't make it, but he found new love with Andrea – but that's in part a coping strategy, a salve for the worry he feels as a parent in a world where your child is truly in danger every moment of every day.

It also helps that he's a tough sonuvabitch, too – and pretty handy with a weapon. His time as a cop has gifted him with a series of skills that transfer alarmingly well to the new world, and also mark him out as a genuine authority figure and *de facto* leader. He is by nature an everyman, a straightforward kind of guy with strong values, a solid moral code

and productive work ethic. In a screwed-up way, the disaster has enabled him to fulfil his potential – his blue-collar 'dude' personality was being swallowed up in our coddled society.

Rick's perfectly suited to a more basic, tougher existence. He's a man of a bygone era, brought back into sharp relevance. He

even starts to look to the future and feel hope for what is to come. And he still gets to mete out justice, like killing the band of cannibals, the Hunters, who ate dying Dale's leg.

Even losing his own hand hasn't stopped Rick. The only thing that might stop him in his tracks would be the loss of Carl. Luckily, we haven't seen what would happen and let's hope we never have to. With his son dead, Rick would be an empty shell of his former self, wandering the world like a walker in waiting. As long as he has Carl, he's as tough as Aron Ralston, the climber who hacked off his own arm to get free of a boulder and certain death. Rick is an alpha survivor.

CARL GRIMES

FIRST APPEARANCE: ISSUE TWO
(ALTHOUGH HE DOES APPEAR IN A FAMILY PORTRAIT IN ISSUE ONE)

There's nothing like being taught to fire a gun at seven years old to make you grow up fast. But thankfully, Carl comes from good stock.

Youth is also on his side, and the resilience of the young to adapt to extreme situations should never be underestimated. Before long, he's saved his mother from a walker, killed Shane to save his dad, survived a gunshot wound, lost his mother and baby sister, and his right eye. Is it any wonder he's no longer a moral little kid? This hardened young boy readily makes independent decisions to protect the other survivors, like killing Ben when we learn he's murdered his own brother, Billy.

He's clearly his father's son, but is on an accelerated track, exposed to mammoth amounts of violence and death very quickly. There's no doubt it will toughen him up, but he may lament the lack of empathy that his father still holds onto when dealing with other survivors in the long run.

SOPHIA

> SOPHIA IS MAINLY A PROTECTED SURVIVOR, THE KEY TO HER SURVIVAL BEING ADAPTATION TO PARENTAL FIGURE AFTER PARENTAL FIGURE.

PELETIER

FIRST APPEARANCE: ISSUE TWO

She may no longer be with us in AMC's TV show, but Sophia is still going strong in the comic (unlike her mother, Carol). Sophia is mainly a protected survivor, the key to her survival being adaptation to parental figure after parental figure. This, combined with a level of denial that helps her deal with the death of most of the people she loves, has made her a survivor.

She's good friends with Carl, which helps, but she isn't cut from the same cloth as the Grimes, being more of a Forrest Gump – present at key events but not active in them. She even went catatonic for a time and actively called caregivers Maggie and Glenn "mother" and "father."

Thankfully, she reveals that she does remember her real mother, even though her multiple suicide attempts and greater affection for Tyreese were traumatic. Ultimately, she's a survivor by attrition. As long as she's allied to someone like Maggie – or even Carl – then she's as protected as anyone can be.

ANDREA

FIRST APPEARANCE: ISSUE TWO (ONE PAGE AFTER SOPHIA)

Andrea may be a hardboiled survivor who's handy with a gun and sports dramatic facial scars, but she's also Rick's current partner and it seems that forming an attachment/alliance with Rick does increase your odds of making it through more issues of the comic (although not so much for Jessie).

The former law firm clerk and sister to college student Amy has been through real rites of passage in the pages of *The Walking Dead*, but she was already known to be headstrong and self-reliant before she had to kill her own sister to prevent her from turning into a walker. Add the discovery that she was a crack shot to that kind of steely willpower and Andrea was a strong candidate for survival long before she got together with Rick. Previously partnered with Dale, she even took on parenting duties for Billy and Ben for a while, when their father Allen died, and taught other survivors how to shoot.

Like her current beau, the post-disaster world has been in many ways the making of her and they truly are kindred spirits. With that kind of bond, Andrea has the skills, temperament and purpose to keep on surviving.

A CRACK SHOT WITH STEELY WILLPOWER, ANDREA WAS A STRONG CANDIDATE FOR SURVIVAL LONG BEFORE SHE GOT TOGETHER WITH RICK.

MAGGIE GREENE

FIRST APPEARANCE: ISSUE 10

All the necessary traits to stay alive were already on display in Hershel Greene's second daughter before the dead got up and walked. She was a fiercely independent rebel, not fitting into society's pre-set roles; she was a liberated thinker; and an experienced loner. Her father gave her the knowledge and resilience to carve out an existence in the harsh new world – Hershel famously barricaded the Greenes into their home, living off what the farm could provide.

When Glenn entered her life, another piece of the survival puzzle was put in place – someone to live for. Alas, she was further tested by the deaths of her father, two sisters and brother. And she almost failed, trying to hang herself, only to be saved by Glenn and Abraham. But, in the end, nature has its way of forcing you to carry on, and Maggie's biological clock has became very insistent. Not only does she take over mothering duties for the orphaned Sophia, but she ably becomes a single parent when Glenn is killed by the Saviors (in front of her, no less).

Now possessing a strong seam of pragmatic stoicism running through her very core, Maggie is an obvious leader for the Hilltop, given what she's been through and her natural role as a mother figure for many. Death is always close, and her awareness of that, and her love for her 'children' make her a powerful force for life in a world of death.

NOW POSSESSING A STRONG SEAM OF PRAGMATIC STOICISM, MAGGIE IS AN OBVIOUS LEADER FOR THE HILLTOP.

WRAMM!

YOU ABOUT **READY?** I'M GIVING YOU GUYS SOME LOW CALIBER GUNS SO THEY'LL BE A LITTLE **EASIER** TO HANDLE.

LET'S DO IT!

YEAH. THIS'LL BE **FUN!**

PKOW!

SURPRISE DIES!

Of course, anyone who is still alive in the comic has lived through the entire zombie outbreak, and shown that they too have the survival instinct, even the Hilltop's cowardly Gregory. However, the comic has introduced us to a few characters who had 'survivor' written all over them, right up to the point when they died…

TYREESE

Athletic, strong, good with a hammer, Tyreese seemingly was an unstoppable force in the comic, until a foolhardy attack plan went horribly wrong and he ended up being captured and ultimately murdered by the Governor. In truth, he never did quite recover mentally from the death of his daughter, Julie, who died in a suicide pact gone wrong. Does Tyreese represent Rick if he was to lose Carl?

LORI

Perhaps not the most natural survivor in terms of skillset, we still felt Lori was safe simply because she had her husband Rick to protect her. No such luck! She was gunned down by one of the Governor's 'soldiers' in 'Made To Suffer.' It remains probably the most shocking death in the entire series.

ABRAHAM

A squaddie through and through, Abraham was very much the 'poster boy' survivor until he was shot through the eye with a crossbow bolt. The almost casual nature of his death, in mid-sentence, while out for a walk with Eugene – as opposed to Tyreese and Glenn's drawn out (no pun intended) death scenes – truly underlines writer Robert Kirkman's *Walking Dead* philosophy: no one is safe.

GLENN

The multi-talented Glenn looked all set for a long life in the series – and in truth he lasted 99 issues – mainly due to a talent for survival and a greater lust for life than any other character (remember, he taught Rick how to forage and avoid the walkers). All of which made his death at the hands of Negan all the more shocking. We're still not quite over it, in truth…

MICHONNE

MICHONNE IS A WALKING METAPHOR FOR HER OLD IDENTITY: A CUTTHROAT LITIGATOR WHO LOST ALL HER LOVED ONES, LIVING AN ALIENATED EXISTENCE.

However, she only gained true survivor status once she bonded with Rick and Carl – protecting Carl gave her a surrogate family, mirroring Rick's survival instinct. She had lovers, too, but they never lasted long – and we don't mean that they broke up – and reflected her divisive nature (she tends to take what she wants, with little heed to repercussions).

If she didn't respect Rick and care for Carl, it's very likely she'd still be alone in the wilderness. And that usually ends one way in the long run in *The Walking Dead*... With her toughness welded to a maternal purpose, Michonne has gained the full range of traits to really go the distance. •

FIRST APPEARANCE: ISSUE 19

Some things are clichés because they're true. And if you were going to put money on anybody surviving until the bitter end, it'd be Michonne. From the first time we saw her – katana in hand, towing two armless, jawless chained zombies in her wake – you knew she was someone not to be trifled with.

It's no surprise to discover that Michonne's pre-disaster life had been no picnic, making her segue to sword-wielding zombie slaughteress easier than most. She became a walking metaphor for her old identity – a cutthroat litigator who lost all her loved ones, living an alienated existence. When she hooked up with the group she still 'spoke' to her dead boyfriend (something she has in common with Rick, who would 'call' his dead wife, Lori). This is the kind of creative coping strategy that allows people to live – a sane insanity that brings cathartic release from the trauma around her.

CLASH OF THE TITANS

When two giants of *The Walking Dead* meet, you can expect the sparks to fly. This time around, Rick and Abraham throw down after Maggie attempts to find relief at the end of a rope.
WORDS: Dan Auty

WHAT'S THE BEEF?
A traumatized, grieving Maggie attempts suicide and is found hanging from a tree. Convinced she is dead, Abraham and his gun prepare to ensure she doesn't return.

ROUND ONE!
Seconds later, Abraham finds himself at the end of a gun barrel, as Rick steps behind him, his pistol raised, saying: "You pull your trigger and I'll pull mine."

ROUND TWO!
Abraham is not easily scared, and attempts to reason with Rick. But he misunderstands his intentions, thinking him simply too

weak to put a bullet through a friend's head. Rick's reluctance is based on the same instinct that has kept him alive for so long – not racing into decisions that could have cataclysmic consequences. "What if she isn't dead?"

ROUND THREE!
Seconds later, Maggie wakes up. Glenn rushes to her, Rick lowers his gun and we

see Abraham consumed by a mix of emotions that are clearly rare for him – surprise, remorse, and even fear. It's a rare moment in Abe's life in the comic.

THE DECIDING BLOW
Hours later, as Abe comes to relieve Rick on night watch, the former soldier attempts to reassert his authority, making it clear that Rick is not his leader. "Right or wrong, next time you point a gun to my head, I'll kill you." Rick's position is equally clear: "Next time you make me put a gun to your head, I won't hesitate to blow your brains out."

AND THE WINNER IS…
Rick, by an inch. Having such strong natural leaders on the same side was always going to lead to a few confrontations, but the fact that Rick essentially saved Maggie's life by standing up to the more impulsive Abraham gives him this one.

THE SECRET DIARY OF A WALKER

It's not easy being a zombie in *The Walking Dead* world, as our week in the life/death of an undead walker shows. Diary entries transcribed by Dan Auty…

MONDAY
Went to the office early. Busy week ahead – calls to make, deals to close, interns to eat. The place was a complete mess – I always knew the cleaners were lazy, but this was ridiculous. Bins overturned, windows broken, internal organs all over the floor.

TUESDAY
I had a power lunch with a broker, but our usual spot was lacking any of my favorites – spleen salad, intestine Niçoise, eyeball sushi. I was going to offer him a job, but his table manners were disgusting, drooling brains all over the tablecloth.

WEDNESDAY
Apparently, I have to go on some team-building day on Friday to develop my business strengths. I know mine already. I'm a great multi-tasker – no one can secure a deal while disemboweling a rival as efficiently as me.

THURSDAY
Brushing up on my corporate business-speak for tomorrow's exercise. Apparently "head-hunting" and "chewing his ear off" have different meanings to what I'd been led to believe.

FRIDAY
This team-building day was as bad as expected. I was paired with Dave from tech support, who clearly has never spoken to a woman before – alive or otherwise – and he smelt just awful. We had to do this exercise in a field, and believe me, my $2,000 suit is *not* made for the countryside. We bonded briefly when we spotted some normos and went over for a 'chat,' but unfortunately this big guy with a funny moustache got a bit carried away with his pitchfork. I'm staying in the city next time, much less dangerous.

Shhhhh....!
TWDM'S Guide To The Whisperers

On the TV show, Rick and the gang are dealing with the danger posed by the Wolves and now Negan, but in the comic there's a new enemy that threatens the safety of Alexandria, the Hilltop, the Sanctuary, and the Kingdom: the Whisperers. *TWDM* assesses the situation with an in-depth look at these silent enemies.
WORDS: Dan Auty

After 11 years and over 150 issues, it can't always be easy for Robert Kirkman to think up new villains. Not so much walkers – they remain as much of a threat as ever, albeit an increasingly rotten one – but the human menace, since people have long been established as the true bad guys of *The Walking Dead*.

Walkers might present a persistent danger, but they are predictable and relatively easy to deal with, if you know what you're doing. Other people, however, are neither predictable nor easy. Never mind food or ammunition, trust is the hardest thing to find in this world. By the time we reach the time jump of issue 127, a strong community has been built in Alexandria and the Hilltop – strangers are rightly treated with suspicion and the community seems well-equipped to deal with threats, be they living or dead. That is, until the Whisperers make their presence known.

WHERE THEY GO?

SILENT THREAT

The Whisperers are not like the Saviors, Scavengers, Hunters, the Governor's army, or any of *The Walking Dead*'s other violent, villainous groups. Indeed, when we first meet them, we don't even know they are human.

The first encounter comes in issue 130. Marco and Ken are trying to get back to the Hilltop, following an accident in which Ken has hurt his leg and loses his horse.

With the rain pelting down and a herd of walkers heading their way, the pair hide in a ditch, while the walkers stumble by them above. Suddenly, they start to hear something unexpected and terrifying… whispered voices, asking, "Where did they go?" When Marco finally makes it back to Hilltop – without Ken – he tells the rest of the survivors what he had heard: "It was the dead. They were speaking."

The next encounter is no less strange. A search party led by Dante is dispatched to try to find Ken, and they too are set upon by

"We whisper and the dead don't mind."
Unknown Whisperer

THERE WERE WHISPERS AND I WAS AFRAID.

IT WAS THE DEAD.

THEY WERE SPEAKING.

walkers. Walkers armed with knives, that is, who tell Dante: "We whisper and the dead don't mind."

The issue ends with Dante beheading one of these creatures, and realizing the zombie's face is merely a mask. The truth of the Whisperers is revealed: these are humans, using the skin of the dead to move freely among them.

BLENDING IN

While it is clearly a gruesome thing to have to endure – wearing dead flesh upon your face for hours on end – there is a logic to the Whisperers' choice of headwear. Throughout the course of *The Walking Dead*, characters have been forced to make unpleasant decisions in order to survive, decisions that anyone from the civilized, pre-apocalyptic world might find abhorrent.

As early as issue four, Rick and Glenn used the rotting goo from expired walkers to disguise their smell as they moved through the streets of Atlanta. And Michonne's method of protection was to have her undead boyfriend and his best friend chained to her, their stench keeping walkers at bay, their jaws and arms removed to ensure her own safety. The Whisperers have only taken these tactics one step further, and attempted to not just blend in with the zombies, but to somehow become them.

Unfortunately for those they encounter, the Whisperers don't want just to hide from the walkers, they also want to kill humans. Their walker disguises enable them to get close to their prey. While walkers are a threat, those experienced at dealing with them, like many of the Hilltop and Alexandria's soldiers, will allow a walker to get close so that they can be dispatched with a blade, rather than wasting a precious bullet and attracting more zombies with the sound of a gunshot. As Jesus and the group he is leading discover in issue 133, if a group of supposed walkers suddenly pull out knives in close proximity, things can get very bloody very quickly.

> ### "They protect us… and we protect them… We live together or we don't live at all." Lydia

LIFE AMONG THEM

But what do the Whisperers want? Is it purely to kill and conquer, or is there some greater goal?

The first insight into their motivation comes when the Whisperer Lydia is captured and taken back to the Hilltop, following the attack on Jesus. Under interrogation, she explains the reasoning behind the dead skin: it is not just protection, but a strange respect for the dead, an acknowledgement that humans are now living in their world.

"We travel with them," she tells Jesus. "They protect us… and we protect them. That is all that is left for us in this world. For us to live and them to not. We live together or we don't live at all."

Jesus's surprise that a 16-year-old girl is being used as a frontline soldier is met with a response that is both chilling and strangely logical. "There are no children anymore. Childhood was always a myth about the illusion of safety. It was a luxury we could no longer afford." This philosophy, the idea that

if you have made it this far then it is because you have let go of any previous notions of a child's place in society, is a long way from Rick's community's attempts to maintain a level of civilization and normality.

But it is partly true, even if Jesus, Rick, Maggie and the others would hate to admit it. In the previous issue, Carl nearly killed two boys with a shovel – the act is in self-defense, but the ferocity of his attack would, in a past life, have seen him locked up for a long time. Now he is barely punished at all.

Lydia *is* still a child, however, and the subsequent conversations she has with Carl reveal that this outlook is really just a result of mental and physical manipulation. "I've never been alone like this," she tells him. "We never split up into anything other than a small group. I'm just so scared."

Even worse, Lydia later tells Carl that she was treated as a sexual plaything for the men in the group: rape was clearly a regular part of her day-to-day existence as a Whisperer.

ALPHA (FE)MALE

It is near the end of issue 138 that the rest of the Whisperers are properly introduced. A trade is proposed – Lydia for the return of captured Dante and Ken – and we learn the identity of their leader. She is a woman, has a shaved head and calls herself Alpha. She states that she is also Lydia's mother.

This initial encounter between Maggie and Alpha reveals the true reason for the Whisperers' first attack on the members of the Hilltop community. They regard the area around their camp as their land, and consider the presence of others upon that land an intrusion. Their initial demand that the Hilltop residents stay out of this territory is all very well, but with no real idea of what they consider "their land," there is a constant risk of accidental incursions.

"We know they're unforgiving of us entering whatever they consider their territory," Maggie says, when she

realizes that Carl has gone after Lydia, who he has become quite attached to.

Alpha and her followers do eventually mark out their territory, making it quite

clear where the Hilltop's land stops and theirs begins. And they do it in the most brutal way – kidnapping and beheading multiple residents, among them Ezekiel, Rosita, and Carl's friend, Josh, and lining their reanimated severed heads up on stakes to create a macabre dividing line.

"I have marked our border. You will know it when you see it," Alpha had told Rick beforehand. No kidding!

"There are no children anymore. Childhood was always a myth about the illusion of safety. It was a luxury we could no longer afford." **Lydia**

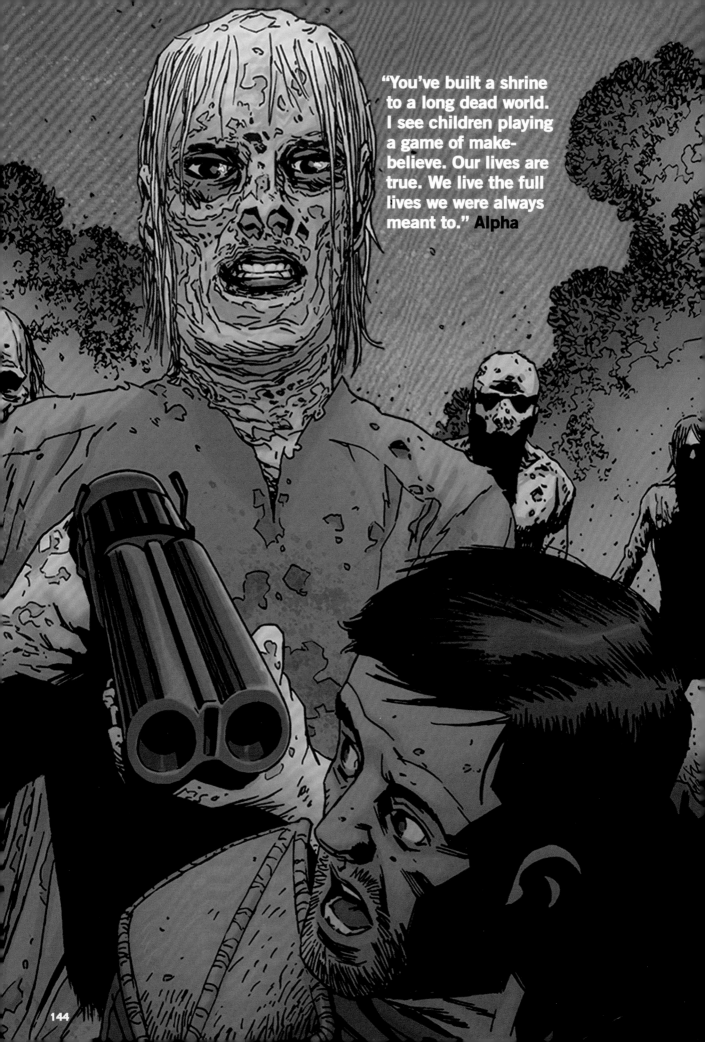

"You've built a shrine to a long dead world. I see children playing a game of make-believe. Our lives are true. We live the full lives we were always meant to." Alpha

"I've never been alone like this. We never split up into anything other than a small group. I'm just so scared." Lydia

DANGEROUS NEIGHBORS

During Rick's encounter with Alpha and the Whisperers' camp, to negotiate the return of both Carl and Lydia, he sees the full extent of both Alpha's belief system, but also a surprising moment of vulnerability. At first, Alpha lays out the way that she and her followers view the world; the old society has gone, and those, like Rick, who strive to return to it, are fools.

"You've built a shrine to a long dead world," she tells him. "I see children playing a game of make-believe. Our lives are true. We live the full lives we were always meant to." Alpha claims that her people are free, and that her role as leader is merely to maintain order, and she will only do it until someone else takes that role.

While we know little about Alpha and her pre-apocalypse role as a mother, there is a moment that suggests that she hasn't entirely left it all behind. Lydia tells her bluntly that she will no longer tolerate the abuse at the hands of the Whisperer men, and

"I have marked our border. You will know it when you see it." Alpha

that she needs to be with Carl's people. Although Alpha's initial response is that such emotion is simple weakness, her whispered command to Rick moments later tells another story: "I can't offer my daughter the life she needs. Not here. Not safely. But you can."

What this ultimately says about Alpha, the Whisperers, and their relationship with the rest of the survivors is unknown. Within a few pages of Alpha's confession to Rick, he discovers the heads of his friends on poles, all the work of this same woman. Rick is cautious about immediately declaring war on the Whisperers – even though he knows something has to be done. But the others in the community are quick to demand revenge, using Lydia as leverage. How much Alpha truly cares for her daughter will soon become evident, but one thing is clear – there is no way that the Whisperers and their neighbors are going to be able to live alongside each other for very long. •

PHOTO: Jamie Parreno.

KILLER IMAGE

It's been a decade since Rick Grimes and co entered our lives in *The Walking Dead* comic book. It's a great landmark for any indie comic and a fantastic achievement for its publisher, Image Comics. *TWDM* couldn't think of any better way to review the comic's history than by chatting to Image head honcho, Eric Stephenson.

INTERVIEW: Martin Eden

riginally founded in 1992 by seven of the leading lights from the comic book world, Image Comics decided to take on the big boys at their own game with such hits as Todd McFarlane's *Spawn*, Erik Larsen's *Savage Dragon* and Jim Lee's *WildC.A.T.s*. Over the next few years, Image became the biggest independent publisher in the business and third biggest in the US behind Marvel and DC Comics, a position it still maintains today.

Since those heady early days, personnel may have changed (including the addition of Robert Kirkman as a partner in 2008) and more titles may have been added (top sellers *Invincible*, *Witchblade* and *Astro City* among them), but Image's remit to publish the very best of creator-owned properties has remained the same. Its current publisher is Eric Stephenson, who has had a long and illustrious comic book career, as *TWDM* finds out…

You became the publisher of Image Comics in 2008. Can you give us a little background on your career before this?

Sure. I started out as [writer/artist and Image co-founder] Jim Valentino's assistant when Image was first formed in 1992, then wrote and edited comics for [writer/artist] Rob Liefeld's Extreme Studios. When Rob was no longer at Image, Extreme became Awesome Entertainment, and I edited books there as well, before doing a little freelance work at Marvel and DC Comics.

Around the same time, I became the managing editor for NextPlanetOver.com's comics content. NPO was a victim of the dotcom bust though, and in the wake of that, I returned to Image as director of marketing in 2001. I remained in that role until 2004, when I was promoted to executive director to work alongside incoming publisher Erik Larsen. Four years later, Erik stepped down and the job was offered to me.

"ZOMBIE COMICS WERE A DEAD END IN 2003, BUT ROBERT CREATED AN ENGAGING CHARACTER DRAMA AGAINST A ZOMBIE APOCALYPSE BACKDROP."

The Walking Dead has been published for 13 years now. What do you think is the secret of its success?

Generally speaking, I would say it's because it focuses more on the people than on the zombies.

A lot of people are surprised to learn that Image originally wasn't all that interested in *The Walking Dead*. Something that's been kind of covered up by the book's success is that zombie comics were a bit of a dead end in 2003. Robert managed to create an engaging character drama against the backdrop of a zombie apocalypse, and I think it's for the characters that people come back to it. If it was just pure zombie mayhem every issue, I'm not sure the book would have lasted as long as it has.

Kirkman has said that he would like to carry the series on for as long as possible. How do you see its future going? Any spin-off comics?

Absolutely not. *The Walking Dead* is available in multiple formats, but Robert has made it very clear he has no intention of ever doing a spin-off.

Why do you think Image Comics is the right place for this series?

Well, aside from the fact that Image believed in Robert enough at the start of his career to do nearly half a dozen series with him – *Tech Jacket*, *Invincible*, *Brit*, *Cloudfall*, *Capes* – before *The Walking Dead* took off, Image offers an unprecedented amount of creative freedom that has definitely worked in the series' favor over the last 10 years.

I think a lot of what Robert has accomplished at Image, not just with *The Walking Dead*, but also with things like *Invincible*, *Super Dinosaur*, and *Thief Of Thieves*, would have been nitpicked and second-guessed anywhere else. And even though other publishers do their own kind of creator-owned comics, something like *The Walking Dead* would have always been a distant priority behind things like *Spider-Man*, *Avengers*, *X-Men*, *Superman*, *Batman*, *Star Wars*, and *GI Joe*.

IMAGE RIGHTS

TWDM's resident comic book fanatic Tom Williams picks his top 10 iconic series to date from Image Comics (not including *The Walking Dead*)…

CHEW
(JUN 2009-PRESENT)
John Layman and Rob Guillory's acclaimed Eisner award-winning series might not follow your average comic plot, but that's what Image is all about. Chronicling the food-related adventures of a super-powered FDA agent, the title has been lauded for its hilarious character-driven storylines.

INVINCIBLE
(JAN 2003-PRESENT)
Another Robert Kirkman creation, *Invincible* follows an adolescent alien adventurer as he struggles to come to grips with his emerging powers and origins. It's one of Image's flagship titles in its superhero line.

THE MAXX
(MAR 1993-AUG 1998)
Difficult to describe and even harder to comprehend, Sam Kieth's surrealist superhero title represents Image's first foray into the realm of the obscure. Flicking between depressing reality and an intoxicating alt-world, its creative use of landscapes and psychoanalysis is delightfully innovative.

PHONOGRAM
(AUG 2006-PRESENT)
Another gem, *Phonogram*'s marriage of music and magic offers a refreshing alternative to the cape and tights approach. Creators Kieron Gillen and Jamie McKelvie cram all the best bits of the Britpop and indie rock genres into their contemporary fantasy setting.

POWERS
(APR 2000-PRESENT)
Brian Michael Bendis and Michael Avon Oeming's cult series juxtaposes standard superhero tropes with a gritty, police-procedural setting. It's won numerous awards, and an FX TV series is reportedly in the works.

Who is (or was) your own favorite character in the comic?
At the moment, Negan is my favorite character, primarily because his dialogue is over-the-top. I can tell Robert has a lot of fun writing him, because Negan just has the most outrageously filthy mouth.

Do you have any say in the storylines/direction of *The Walking Dead*, and have you ever requested any changes?
Nope. That's completely antithetical to how Image works. Robert and I have the kind of relationship where he'll tell me about what's happening in upcoming issues, and if something sounds strange to me, I'll question the reasoning behind it. But no, Robert has the final say.

That's how Image was set up way back in 1992, and I think that hands-off attitude works to Robert's, as well as other creators' benefits. Robert knows what he's doing with his books. Brian K Vaughan knows what he's doing with *Saga*. Ed Brubaker knows how to write *Fatale*. Grant Morrison, Jonathan Hickman, Howard Chaykin, John Layman, Greg Rucka – these are some of the best writers in all of comics. They don't need me to tell them how to do their jobs.

If a new creator has an idea for a comic, how would they go about approaching Image with it? What does Image look for in a project?
People generally email their pitches to me, but we still get a lot at conventions or through the mail.

In terms of what we're looking for… Well, we're always on the lookout for something different. It's like, *The Walking Dead* is a successful zombie comic, so

"THE MORE INVENTIVE AND UNIQUE THE PROJECT, THE BETTER CHANCE A NEW CREATOR HAS TO GRAB IMAGE COMICS' ATTENTION."

SAGA
(MAR 2013-PRESENT)
Brought to life by Fiona Staples' jaw-dropping inks and pencils, Brian K Vaughan's space opera/fantasy title has proved to be one of Image's best earners, with issue one selling through five separate printings.

SAVAGE DRAGON
(1992-PRESENT)
Often cited as one of the greatest comic heroes of all time, Erik Larsen's eponymous, green-skinned amnesiac

superhero was one of Image's debut characters. The series stands alone as the longest-running US full color comic book to feature a single artist/writer. Not bad going, huh?

SPAWN
(MAY 1992-PRESENT)
A Todd McFarlane creation, this dark, occult-orientated superhero series was an instant hit, with the debut issue selling a record 1.7 million copies. A feature film, HBO animated series, and toyline followed.

WITCHBLADE
(NOV 1995-PRESENT)
One of Mark Silvestri's premier Top Cow titles, *Witchblade* – a fantasy series centered around a mysterious sentient artifact – has enjoyed tremendous success since its mid-90s launch.

YOUNGBLOOD
(APRIL 1992-PRESENT)
Controversial creator Rob Liefeld's superhero series, Image Comics' first release, debuted as the highest-selling independent comic book ever.

SHIT, I DIDN'T KNOW THERE WERE THIS MANY OUT HERE.

PIECE OF CAKE.

"NEGAN IS MY FAVORITE CHARACTER, PRIMARILY BECAUSE HIS DIALOGUE IS OVER-THE-TOP. HE HAS THE MOST OUTRAGEOUSLY FILTHY MOUTH."

WHO DARES TRESPASS ON THE SOVEREIGN LAND OF—

OH, SHIT— JESUS? IS THAT YOU?!

IN CASE YOU HAVEN'T CAUGHT ON...

I JUST SLID MY DICK DOWN YOUR THROAT...

AND YOU THANKED ME FOR IT.

THIS PAGE, OPPOSITE PAGE & OVER: A selection of images from recent issues of *The Walking Dead* comic book. Negan (this page, top right) is one of Stephenson's favorite characters in the series.

CARL, RUN INSIDE BEFORE THEY BLOCK THE WAY— GO!

SWASH!

we've kind of got that covered. We do another zombie book, '68, that had an interesting twist in it that was set against the backdrop of the Vietnam War, but that's kind of an anomaly. I don't know that we'd necessarily do another zombie book after that. Same with superhero books – the market is riddled with them and it's just more difficult to stand out in the crowd.

I think that's how people like Jonathan Hickman or The Luna Brothers or Justin Jordan made such a huge impression on me with their submissions. With Hickman, his initial book was *The Nightly News* and it was unlike anything else I'd seen up to that point. Every book he's done for Image since then has been different – his

new series *East Of West* is nothing like *The Nightly News* or *The Manhattan Projects* or *Pax Romana*.

Or something like *Chew* – John Layman pitched this book about a detective who gets visions from the food he eats, and it's set in this world where chicken has been outlawed. There'd never been anything like that before and it's almost impossible to categorize.

The more inventive and unique the project, the better chance a new creator has to grab our attention.

Do you have any advice for aspiring comic creators?
Stop talking about what you're going to do and do it. Actions really do speak louder than words, and the best way to get going in comics is to sit down and start making them.

What's the average day like for the publisher at Image? For example, what will you be doing today?
A lot of talking! Communication is a big part of the job, so yes, there's a lot of talking and a lot of emailing. I have a conference

"ACTIONS REALLY DO SPEAK LOUDER THAN WORDS. THE BEST WAY TO GET GOING IN COMICS IS TO SIT DOWN AND START MAKING THEM."

call with a writer and artist team I'm really excited about working with this afternoon; the writer has worked with Image before, but the artist has been under contract at another publisher and is eager to get the lay of the land here.

That's a pretty standard aspect of the job – recruiting talent, discussing contracts, mapping out publishing plans for the months ahead. We're well into 2014 with some of our planning, and that's really exciting.

Beyond that, there's a lot of standard business – setting print-runs, getting things ready to be solicited in Diamond's *Previews* catalogue, looking over books before they come out. Mark Millar and Frank Quitely's *Jupiter's Legacy* #1 is on my desk at the moment, for instance, and that's pretty cool. There are numerous aspects of my job that honestly seem kind of mundane to me, but then I look at something like that – reviewing the first issue of an all-new Mark Millar/Frank Quitely comic – and it's like, 'No, this job rocks!'

What are your views on digital comics and the future of print comics?
Digital comics are definitely becoming a bigger part of our business, and I think it's great that guys like Brian K Vaughan and Marcos Martin can launch something like *The Private Eye* on their own and have it become an immediate sensation.

That said, I'm happy to report that print sales are more robust for us than ever, so I'm optimistic that there will ultimately be a place for both.

Is there a current hidden gem at Image – a comic book that isn't getting the attention it deserves?
Depends on what you're looking for. If you're a zombie fanatic, as I said, we do the '68 series. I think for anyone not aware of that, it might be a bit of a surprise.

Beyond that, Richard Starkings' *Elephantmen* series hits issue 50 in a few months and I think that's one of the best and most inventive sci-fi books on the market. The world-building in that book is second to none and, over the years, Richard has worked with some truly incredible artists.

Similarly, I think Erik Larsen is still doing something really special with *Savage Dragon*. I know a lot of people tend to dismiss it as standard superhero punch-up

> # "THERE ARE ASPECTS OF MY JOB THAT ARE MUNDANE, BUT THEN I GET TO REVIEW THINGS LIKE THE FIRST ISSUE OF AN ALL-NEW MARK MILLAR/FRANK QUITELY COMIC – AND IT'S LIKE, 'NO, THIS JOB ROCKS!'"

comics, but there's actually much more to it than that, starting with the fact that the characters have aged in real time, so that 21 years have passed since Dragon first woke up naked and bereft of memory in a burning field. Issue 193, out this Fall, will actually signal a major change in the series that is fairly unprecedented. I think what Erik does takes a lot of vision and a lot of guts.

Any hints or sneak peeks at upcoming hot Image projects?
I think everyone's going to want to check out Greg Rucka and Michael Lark's *Lazarus* this June. We're running a preview for that in *The Walking Dead* #109, and it's going to be amazing.

If you had to pick out one single favorite Image issue or series from Image's history – not including *The Walking Dead* – what would you choose?
Saga.

Finally, what have been your favorite moments of *The Walking Dead* TV show? Are you involved with the creation of it at all?
Nope. Image is 100 per cent uninvolved in the television show – that's Robert's baby.

My favorite thing about the show, honestly, is just watching how the storyline diverges from that of the comics. I think it's great that the show can surprise long-time fans of the comic book, and I look forward to seeing how they continue to push the boundaries with that sort of thing. •

Find out more about Image Comics at: www.imagecomics.com

CLASH OF THE TITANS

When giants of *The Walking Dead* meet, you can expect sparks to fly. This time, Hershel takes on the Grimes in a classic case of "Get off my land!"

WORDS: Dan Auty

WHAT'S THE BEEF?

Rick and the group have been staying on Hershel's farm while Carl recovers from being shot. While preparing to move into the barn, Rick asks Hershel if they could live in the house instead.

ROUND ONE!

Not only does Hershel not want them in his house, he makes it clear that once Carl is better they must leave entirely. Which is news to our hero, who had presumed they were now permanent residents.

ROUND TWO!

If Rick isn't happy about this, then Lori *really* isn't happy. She confronts Hershel,

who is adamant that the loss of both of his sons the day before means that more than ever he must protect his own family. Lori sees it otherwise: "If we hadn't been here and given you extra guns you'd all be dead right now!"

ROUND THREE!

As the argument moves into more personal territory, Hershel raises his hand to strike Lori – much to the shock of just about

everyone, including Hershel himself. Before that happens, Rick steps in and attempts to appeal to Hershel's sense of humanity.

THE DECIDING BLOW

Hershel makes his point even more forcefully by pressing a gun to Rick's head. Otis is horrified and forces Hershel back, but this is clearly the end of the debate. "Fine. We'll leave," says Rick. "We're leaving."

AND THE WINNER IS…

On the face of it, Hershel. He got what he wanted. But hours later, he confesses to Otis that he is appalled by his actions, clearly driven by his grief. "I think I've lost my mind," he states. And ultimately, he reconciles with Rick and moves his family to the greater safety of the prison.

THE SECRET DIARY OF A WALKER

It's not easy being a zombie in *The Walking Dead* world, as our week in the life/death of an undead walker shows. Diary entries transcribed by Dan Auty…

MONDAY

Not a great start to the week… It was still dark when I woke up. I was halfway through a dream about a helicopter. Something smelled funny, like the inside of a dirty old box. That's when I realized I was inside a dirty old box.

TUESDAY

Good news and bad news today. On the upside, I got out of the box for a few minutes. Some normo with a ridiculous moustache kept talking away to no one in particular. I tried to have a nibble on him, but I couldn't get close. That's when I realized the bad

news: I seem to be missing everything from the neck down…

WEDNESDAY

I was finally taken out of the box for good – and dropped into a giant fish tank. I don't know what this moustachioed dude is playing at, but he's one of the rudest normos I've ever met. Does he really think I've got nothing better to do but float around, watching him sit in

an armchair all night? Just wait until I get out of here, dude!

THURSDAY

Getting to know some of my neighbours. Most of them are OK, but there's some guy above me who keeps bobbing up and down on the ceiling of our tank. I'd tell him to keep it down but I think I left my lower jaw in that box.

FRIDAY

Guess I'm gonna be here for a while. We've started playing 'I Spy…' in our tank to pass the time. Unfortunately, the view is a bit limited – G for Glass, C for Chair, R for Rude Moustachioed Normo. Ho-hum!

THE WALKING D-EDITORS

The roles of those who work on a comic book are easily defined: the writer pens the script, the illustrator draws the art, the letterer adds the words, and so on. But what exactly does a comic book *editor* do? *TWDM* puts the question to the current and former *The Walking Dead* editors, Sean Mackiewicz and Sina Grace. WORDS & INTERVIEW: David Bassom

OPPOSITE PAGE, LEFT: Here's a typical page from the comic, featuring Charlie Adlard's artwork and mark-ups by the editor of where the speech balloons should be placed. RIGHT: Here's the same page after it has been fully inked. The process continues with shading and the insertion of the balloons (see over page).

Sina Grace and Sean Mackiewicz truly know how to bring *The Walking Dead* to life. As past and present editors of Robert Kirkman's smash-hit comic book, they have been responsible for ensuring *The Walking Dead* has continued to reach readers each and every month, on time and on stunning form.

"My role is really about making sure that everyone hits their marks and stays on schedule," says Mackiewicz, who has been *The Walking Dead*'s editor since issue 102. "I have to coordinate with the entire creative team – the writers, pencilers, inkers, colorists, letterers – to ensure that everything is flowing as smoothly as possible. And I have to get Robert's views and make sure his decisions are being put into action."

"The role involves the things pretty much all comic book editors do," adds Grace, who as Mackiewicz's predecessor edited issues 72 to 101 over a three-year period. "It involves things like spell-checking, proof-reading, balloon placements (saying where all the comic's word balloons go), and deadline management – keeping in touch with the artists, the printer and the production people. We also have to keep track of various creative things, like continuity. In short, the role involves keeping track of a thousand little things and just making sure everyone's happy and that the ship is running smoothly."

> "WE GET A LOT OF MAIL EVERY MONTH AND IT'S MY JOB TO PICK OUT THE MOST INTERESTING LETTERS – WHETHER THEY CONTAIN PRAISE OR BLIND HATRED."
> SEAN MACKIEWICZ

THE WRITE TO REPLY

Both Mackiewicz and Grace agree that one of the role's most enjoyable aspects is editing 'Letter Hacks,' the comic book's letters pages which allow readers to have their say on all things *Walking Dead*. "We get a lot of mail every month," Mackiewicz explains, "and it's my job to sort through it and pick out the most interesting letters – whether they contain praise or blind hatred. I'll put those together and write the responses to them, and then hand them to Robert. We'll have a little back and forth and then it goes to print.

"The interaction is refreshing in comics," he notes. "You don't see letters pages that often any more. You could argue there's not a need for them any more, with the online fan interaction, but I think it's a unique way to experience a comic book."

"The letters column is a great part of the comic book," Sina Grace agrees. "I think it's a bit of a palette cleanser too, especially when it comes after a particularly intense story. After you finish your experience, it's nice that you can enter a space where you can digest it and communicate with other fans.

"It was really fun to work on," he continues. "Robert loves his fans and there's a great back-and-forth between them that just makes for a more interesting fan experience. The challenge with it is that there are hundreds of letters that come in every month, and it's so hard to pick just a few [for publication]. There were a lot of interesting ones and I would almost feel like a terrible person for not printing a letter, especially when someone would say at the end of their letter, 'This is my second or third time writing.' But you always had to go for the most interesting

THIS PAGE, LEFT: Sina Grace is stunned by the wallpaper behind him. RIGHT: Once the inks have been done, the gray shading is added by Cliff Rathburn. OPPOSITE PAGE, LEFT: Finally the speech balloons are added by letterer Rus Wooton and the page is finished. RIGHT: This is how it all begins – the page in script form.

PHOTOS: Megan Mack.

"ROBERT KIRKMAN LOVES HIS FANS AND THERE'S A GREAT BACK-AND-FORTH BETWEEN THEM THAT JUST MAKES FOR A MORE INTERESTING FAN EXPERIENCE." SINA GRACE

letters and you had to get a balance between 'I love your book' and 'I hate your book.'"

FIRST AND FOREMOST

Mackiewicz and Grace were veterans of the comic book world before they became editors of The Walking Dead. Mackiewicz joined Image Comics from DC Comics, and had also worked on romance, suspense and paranormal titles at Harlequin Books; all of which, he says, gave him invaluable experience of working on projects that have "passionate fan bases." Grace, meanwhile, began his career as an editorial intern at Top Cow and had long been self-publishing his own comic books (which he writes, draws and letters), when he successfully applied for the editorship of The Walking Dead.

Neither Mackiewicz nor Grace needed any introduction to The Walking Dead prior to working on the comic book. Mackiewicz recalls that he had been a fan of the comic from the very beginning: "I picked up Walking Dead issue one way back when – and then sold it prematurely to pay for rent in leaner years!" he admits with a laugh. "When I heard Robert was looking for a new editor, it was nice timing because in the past year, I'd actually just caught up on the three years I missed out on. I was among the many people who jumped back onboard as it was building to issue 100."

Grace, meanwhile, could have been described as a 'lapsed fan' prior to joining the comic. "What I'm about to say is taboo, and Robert knows it, but I had been a reader of The Walking Dead for two years – and then I stopped," he explains. "I was a fan but then I stopped reading the book because I read in an interview that there was no ending in sight and Robert didn't know what the ending is. And I was such a little brat that I decided to stop reading the book, because I had lost faith!

"But when I later found out that The Walking Dead was looking for an editor, I was really excited about the idea of returning to that world and especially working for Robert. Robert, as a figure, is just relentless about the power of creativity

"I THINK EVERYONE IMAGINES THEY'D BE THE HERO OF THE STORY, ALTHOUGH I'M NOT SURE ANYONE WOULD WANT TO BE RICK AT THIS POINT... I DEFINITELY WOULDN'T!"

SEAN MACKIEWICZ

Page 8: five panels

Panel one:
Wide panel: Carl is in the living room of the house, sitting in the foreground, reading. Past him, we see Rick coming downstairs, looking at him.

1   Rick: I'm making lunch.

2   Rick: You want a sandwich?

Panel two:
Wide panel: Stat of Carl in the foreground. He's not looking up from his book, not moving. Rick stands at the foot of the stairs, looking at Carl.

3   Rick: Carl?

Panel three:
Small panel: Just a shot of Carl, not looking up, reading, we're looking at him from Rick's POV now.

Panel four:
Small panel: Close on Rick, looking sternly at Carl.

4   Rick: Damn it, Carl.

5   Rick: Look at me.

Panel five:
Wide panel: Close on Carl, looking up from his book at Rick. He's shooting daggers with his eyes, it's a cold dead stare. He's lost all respect for his father, and we see that here.

and the power of owning your creative properties, and that was so inspiring. I thought 'OK, I just have to do this.'"

THE NEVERENDING STORY

Both editors have their own views on the secret of *The Walking Dead*'s enduring appeal. "It's all down to the characters and a great 'What if?' scenario," Mackiewicz notes. "*The Walking Dead* raises a lot of interesting questions: how would you survive? What would be the changing landscape of this world? And what sacrifices would it demand?"

He continues: "I think everyone would like to imagine they'd be the hero of the story, although I'm not sure anyone would want to be Rick at this point... I wouldn't. I definitely wouldn't! But I think the scenario provides plenty of interesting story opportunities and that really appeals to readers out there."

"Fans are fascinated by the concept – a zombie story that never ends," offers Grace. "Fans are fascinated to see what the apocalypse looks like three months in, four months in, six months in... Not many people have done anything like that. I also think the other secret of the comic's success is that it follows the same set of characters through that time span. I feel that other franchises or other versions of this would veer off at a certain point and sort of follow random threats. Look at *Resident Evil* – they kind of bounce between five or six different characters. But that doesn't happen with *The Walking Dead*."

Mackiewicz and Grace are also united in their views on what *The Walking Dead's* TV adaptation has meant for the comic book. Both are full of praise for the series and recognize it has brought "new

attention" and "a new level of awareness" for the comic book. Grace has also observed how many viewers of the TV show have specifically turned to the comic book in the hope of learning where future storylines may lead. "It was funny, but I'd notice at conventions that whatever was happening in the TV show, people would be looking for the trade paperback set right after the events they'd just seen in the show," Grace explains. "People would come up to me and say, 'OK, they just went to the prison. Show me what happens at the prison.' We'd then have to explain that the TV show is so divergent from the book, and would encourage them to just read the book from the beginning."

"The TV show has been an entry point for a lot of people," Mackiewicz adds.

"I actually have a cousin who is not a comic book reader but got into *The Walking Dead* through the TV show. Now she's emailing me to make sure that, as a mother of a young child, nothing happens to Carl!"

MOVING ON...

Given the enormous – and still growing – popularity of *The Waking Dead*, and the praise he heaps on both the comic and its "brilliant, wonderfully creative" team, it's not surprising to learn that Grace didn't reach the decision to stand down as editor easily. "I was incredibly sad to leave. It was not a quick or even rational decision to make, especially as I left just as season three was about to start and the comic was just getting into this new era of drama with Negan and that storyline. Negan is here to stay, he will carry the same gravitas as The Governor as a character, and that's going to be exciting. But I had an urge to go full steam on some projects I had in the background. I'm still drawing a monthly comic book through Image called *Lil' Depressed Boy* and I just released a graphic novel, *Not My Bag*."

Clearly, Sina Grace feels that he left *The Walking Dead* in good health and is confident readers will remain gripped by its upcoming storylines. And in the long term, both he and Sean Mackiewicz have no doubts there's plenty of life left in *The Walking Dead*.

"Robert will be doing *The Walking Dead* as long as humanly possible," says Grace. "He talks in 50-issue chunks. He has so many ideas and plans for the characters, I'd not be surprised when we are all celebrating the 200th issue."

"Everyone who is involved with the comic enjoys working on it and it's very personal to Robert," Mackiewicz adds. "Robert jokes about doing a thousand issues. So *The Walking Dead* is in no danger of ending any time soon." •

> **"NEGAN IS HERE TO STAY, HE WILL CARRY THE SAME GRAVITAS AS THE GOVERNOR AS A CHARACTER, AND THAT'S GOING TO BE EXCITING."**
> SINA GRACE

A SLAY IN THE LIFE

CURRENT EDITOR SEAN MACKIEWICZ (PICTURED RIGHT) OUTLINES A TYPICAL DAY WORKING ON *THE WALKING DEAD*...

"My day usually starts around 8.30am, when I pop open my email and see what came in overnight. I'd say that's when most of the scripts and new art comes in. So that dictates how the rest of your day will go – be that exceedingly well, or not so well.

"After that, it's a case of doing what needs to be done first – whether that's doing placements [for the balloons] or it's reading scripts and getting notes, or talking to the Skybound team about merchandising opportunities. As well as *The Walking Dead*, I also edit all the other Skybound titles – *Invincible*, *Guarding the Globe*, *Thief of Thieves*, *Clone*, *Witch Doctor: Malpractice* and *Super Dinosaur*. I also look over products that are in development. So, it really is a catch-all position.

"My role involves working with creators from places as far away as Germany and Spain. Because of the time differences, it's not uncommon for me to still be answering emails at nine, 10, 11 o'clock at night.

"The role keeps me interested because of the talent and creativity of the people I work with and the sheer range of the work... I came from superhero books and now I get to work on a couple of superhero books, plus crime, horror and sci-fi. There's never a dull moment."

Mackiewicz laughs at the idea he spends a lot of his time correcting Robert Kirkman's spelling. "Robert's spelling is actually really good," he explains. "I'm a grammar hound, so I can quibble with his usage of commas. But his spelling is exceedingly good."

MAKING A SPLASH

One of the highlights of Charlie Adlard's artwork is his tremendous splash panels (aka full-page or double-page illustrations). Although he uses these splash panels relatively sparingly, when he does do them they are always memorable. *TWDM* looks at our choice of one of his most impactful splashes of the series. WORDS: Dan Auty

How Did We Get Here?

This splash appears in issue 74. Glenn and Heath have traveled from Alexandria to Washington DC to find supplies. Jumping across rooftops, Heath leads Glenn to the alleyway that he usually uses to access the stores on the street. Only this time, it is packed with ravenous walkers.

What's The Scene?

Pictured dramatically from above, Glenn and Heath stare down at the narrow, zombie-infested passageway. Heath's simple dialogue says it all...

No Way Out

Comic book artists don't often have the chance to depict aerial scenes, so Charlie Adlard makes the most of this opportunity. We are used to seeing hordes of walkers approaching head-on, their numbers obscured by their mass, so an overhead shot like this makes for a fascinating and unique splash.

Things Are Looking Down

Adlard uses the expanse of wall to create the effect of dizzying height, the bricks stretching, row after row, down to the ground. The fire escape ladder to the right of Heath seems almost to taunt our heroes, tempting them to make the journey down, while the sparseness of Heath's words lets the visuals do all the talking.

This is also the last time we visit the pair this issue, leaving their fate unknown for another few weeks. Perhaps not quite a cliffhanger, but it's certainly a wall-gripper. •

THE SECRET DIARY OF A WALKER

It's not easy being a zombie in *The Walking Dead* world, as our week in the life/death of an undead walker reveals. Diary entries transcribed by Dan Auty.

MONDAY

Decided this would be a good week to get myself some new clothes. I firmly believe that just because you're dead, it isn't a reason to let your sartorial standards slip. A good suit or dress doesn't always hang well if you lack limbs, but you should at least make an effort.

TUESDAY

Found a nice pair of shoes today — classy, sturdy and in great condition. Once I wipe the brains from the soles and pull the severed foot out of the right one, they'll look as good as new.

WEDNESDAY

Not a great day for this sharp-dressing walker. It rained all day, and then some jawless idiot drooled rancid goo all over my tux. I have, however, heard that there's a bunch of normos nearby, holed up in that old prison. Most of my friends want to head up there to get dinner, but I'm going to see if I can learn some fashion tips from them first. For instance, are sideburns now passé?

THURSDAY

Staggered up to the prison. Not much luck with the normos, but I did find myself a brand new suit — seriously sophisticated. What was *not* sophisticated were my attempts to put it on — rigor mortis doesn't exactly make dressing and undressing easy. But nine hours later, I was dressed to impress.

FRIDAY

Bad day all round. I saw some young, cool-looking normos in the prison yard. I went over to check out their hip, casual style, and see what they thought of my new suit. I got a knife through my head for my troubles. Certainly not the fashion gurus I thought they were. •

"FROM BEFORE I CAN REMEMBER, COMIC BOOKS WERE AROUND THE HOUSE... I REMEMBER MICKEY MOUSE FROM BEFORE I COULD READ."

MONSTERS'
Ink

The start of 'All Out War' marked many changes to *The Walking Dead*, not least in its personnel due to an increase in release frequency of the single issues. New additions to the staff included inker Stefano Gaudiano who joins *TWDM* for a chat about his art, what it's like inking Charlie Adlard and how it feels to be the new boy. INTERVIEW & WORDS: Stuart Barr

THIS PAGE & OPPOSITE: New boy Stefano Gaudiano hard at work on an upcoming issue of *The Walking Dead* comic. Gaudiano compares inking to tracing, but very good tracing.

nker Stefano Gaudiano is a new addition to the tight-knit *Walking Dead* creative team, joining from issue 115 for an epic 12-issue story, 'All Out War,' which has also seen the comic switch to an ambitious bi-monthly publishing schedule.

Italian by birth, Gaudiano's family moved to the US when he was in high school where he began working on fanzines. Inspired by Kevin Eastman and Peter Laird's *Teenage Mutant Ninja Turtles*, a teenage Gaudiano self-published his first comic, a black and white anthology title, with some likeminded friends. At college, he met writer Steven T Seagle and the pair collaborated on the six-issue series *Kafka*, which would go on to be nominated for an Eisner Award (recently republished in trade paperback by Image Comics).

After making his professional debut, Gaudiano went on to work on a number of titles for independent publishers while also working as a commercial artist on animation and games projects. He says: "Eventually I landed at DC Comics, at this stage I was penciling and inking my own work."

While at DC, Gaudiano decided to make the transition from pencils to inks. Speaking frankly, he admits without regret: "I'm a better inker than penciler, basically. I really enjoy it. I like working with other people. My first inking job was *Gotham Central* for DC Comics in 2003 and I did that for a few years. From there, I moved to Marvel and worked on *Daredevil*."

It's clear that working on comics is more than just a way to pay the mortgage and Gaudiano

> "MY ASSUMPTION AS A CHILD WAS THAT COMICS WERE DONE BY MACHINE SOMEHOW. THEN I REALIZED THAT PEOPLE ACTUALLY DRAW THIS."

is an enthusiastic fan of the art form, whose love of the medium goes back to his Italian childhood. "From before I can remember, comic books were around the house," he explains.

Perhaps surprisingly for an artist associated with dark and noir-ish work, it is Walt Disney's most treasured creation that is his formative comics memory. "It was Mickey Mouse… I remember that character from before I could read."

The comic book industry is dominated by English language-speaking countries, but the work of the likes of Hergé, Goscinny, Uderzo, Moebius, Otomo and many others proves there's life beyond the USA and UK. In fact, comic books were so popular in 1970s' Italy that even the Vatican published its own range. This proved to be another major influence on Gaudiano's young imagination: "Within the book, they had a variety of stories, ranging from humor to adventure to educational things. I was constantly exposed to a variety of art styles, genres and stories."

At the same time, more mature comic 'magazines' were finding their way into the household. One of these was the legendary French magazine *Métal Hurlant*, aka *Heavy Metal*. "I was exposed to these amazing artists, like Philippe Druillet and Alberto Breccia. The latter did this series called *Mort Cinder*... I just loved the artwork on that."

Gaudiano credits Marvel for inspiring him to become an artist. "The first time my parents gave me money and said, 'Go get what you want,' I just zeroed in on Spider-Man," remarks Gaudiano, adding that Stan Lee's highly individual and conversational style was key to drawing him in. "That thing he did where he addressed the reader and introduced not only himself but [the artists], giving them nicknames, 'Jazzy' John Romita, it made me think, 'Wow! It's not all done with rubber stamps.'"

Gaudiano laughs at the irony of this adolescent notion in light of his career. "When I saw *Donald Duck*, my assumption was that it was done by machine somehow," he chuckles. "Then all of a sudden, I realized that people actually draw this."

Although Gaudiano had made the transition to working as an inker by the time he came to Marvel, tight scheduling and the commitments of the regular artist did mean he was able to realize a childhood dream and pencil a few pages of *Spider-Man*. "And for once I didn't choke," he says. "One of the problems I've had as a penciler is that I get completely tangled up in all the details. Give me someone else's art and I'll trace it. That's much easier. But

> **"I SEE A LOT OF INKS THAT LEAVE ME COLD. SO I VALUE WHAT I DO A LOT... I THINK IT'S A GREAT CRAFT TO MASTER."**

when it came to *Spider-Man*, I tapped into it, turned around five pages and made the deadline."

Gaudiano has given some thought to the underlying reasons for inking being his true calling as an artist. "I grew up in a family with three brothers," he explains. "I used to like tracing things. I remember being somewhat teased for a drawing that I'd traced, a cover of *Captain America* by Jack Kirby, and one of my older brothers would say, 'Well, you've traced it.' 'Yeah, but look at how well I've traced it.'"

He laughs at the memory.

Does he still face that childhood accusation, that what he does is just tracing? "I totally embrace that actually," he responds immediately. "I don't want to put myself down and I don't want to put any of my fellow inkers down, but I think of it as tracing."

Disarmingly honest, perhaps surprisingly so, Gaudiano is clear that inking is both a craft and a skill. "Looking at Charlie Adlard's art, you can very easily suck the life out of [it] if you don't tap into something within yourself, without putting some level of inspiration into the work.

STEFANO GAUDIANO FACT FILE

NAME: Stefano Gaudiano
PROFESSION: Inker, artist
PLACE OF BIRTH: Italy
BIOGRAPHY: As his name suggests, Stefano Gaudiano is of Italian descent, moving to Denver, Colorado in his teenage years. At the age of 16, he started to self-publish his own comics, which led to his first professional gig, working with writer Steven T Seagle to create the six-issue series *Kafka* (recently republished by Image Comics). He has since worked on a whole host of titles, most notably as inker on *Daredevil*, *Gotham Central* and *X-O Manowar*. He started work on issue 115 of *The Walking Dead* to help ensure the 12-part 'All Out War' meets its bi-weekly schedule.
ARTIST'S BLOG:
stefanogaudiano.blogspot.co.uk

"I see a lot of inks that leave me cold. So I value what I do a lot… I think it's a great craft to master and you can do it well, or you can do it very poorly, but in my mind you can still call it tracing. It's a completely different level of creative investment than penciling. I'll be frank, I've worked with a number of artists who I don't think draw as well as I do, but oh my God, they can put out a story in an interesting way… Being a competent penciler is one of the most difficult jobs that you can have in the commercial art field."

Gaudiano has an interesting analogy to describe his craft: "The most flattering thing I can compare inking to is a singer where someone else has written the song. If you are Frank Sinatra, you are going to just kill it. Sometimes as an inker I've felt like I've been able to take something that might have been mediocre and elevate it into something good. But still, I didn't write the song."

Throughout his time working on *The Walking Dead*, resident artist Charlie Adlard had inked all his own pencils, but, as Gaudiano explains, the ramping up of the publication schedule for 'All Out War' meant help was required.

"Robert Kirkman got in touch and said they were doing this incredible thing, they were going to publish the book twice a month," he states. "Even though Charlie can work insanely fast, it would have been too much for him… and they asked if I was interested."

Clearly he was, with the first few issues featuring

his inks already having hit newsstands (his first issue, 115, was released in October last year), how far in advance of publication does he work? "Not that far actually," he says. "I think I am about three and a half issues ahead of the publishing schedule right now. Considering that it's coming out bi-weekly, I feel like I'm just catching up. I only ask for the scripts at the last possible moment because I don't read ahead, I like to focus on what I am working on."

Despite having contributed to a number of superhero titles in the most recent phase of his career, Gaudiano sees *The Walking Dead* as a natural fit. He says: "A lot of the books that I've worked on were more street level books in the superhero genre, like *Daredevil*. Even though the guy wears a bright shiny costume, there is always something shadowy going on."

Gaudiano reveals that one challenge comes from working with Adlard's amazing pencils. "A lot of the time, when people are

THIS PAGE & OPPOSITE: Some of the more recent ink work of Gaudiano (pictured at his desk, top left). It's not the same as Charlie Adlard's – every artist is different, after all – but it stands up well to comparison.

working on a monthly schedule, you get pencils that are a little bit on the loose side. You have to go in and make certain decisions about how to place blacks or which textures you are going to use. Charlie gets it all worked out in the pencils. My challenge is how not to mess it up… I need to dig a little bit deeper and try not to take away more than I can put back in.

"Technically it is really easy, but it becomes more of a challenge to do something that's greater than just a competent job," he continues. "I feel like it is going to take a few issues before I start flowing with my line work. It's never going to be as good as when Charlie inks himself, but maybe I can play along and bring a little bit more of myself into it without ruining what he's already got."

> **"THE MOST FLATTERING THING I CAN COMPARE INKING TO IS A SINGER WHERE SOMEONE ELSE HAS WRITTEN THE SONG."**

On the flip side, it's been a strange transition for Adlard too, who told *TWDM* at a recent signing of his book, *The Art Of Charlie Adlard*, that having someone else ink his pencils was an unusual experience. Traditionally, he's always inked his own art, but he was slowly getting used to seeing someone else's inks. To flip Gaudiano's earlier analogy, for Adlard, it must be like

writing a personal song and then allowing someone else perform it.

From the readers' point of view, the switch, although understandably noticeable, has not been so obvious as to be detrimental to their enjoyment of the comic. This is a big compliment to Gaudiano's impressive inking.

A fan of *The Walking Dead* beforehand, Gaudiano admits that his new job interferes with his own enjoyment of the story. "I like getting the trades, because they're like potato chips," he explains. "That's been frustrating. I get the art piecemeal, so I get the cliffhangers and have to wait to find out where it's going. I think I know less now than I used to when I was just an average reader of *The Walking Dead*."

One last question before we have to let Gaudiano return to inking the next issue, but it's a good one: have Kirkman and Adlard managed to gross him out yet? "Oh God, yes!" he laughs. "On the issue I'm working on right now, when I saw the conclusion, I shot off an email. What a horrific cliffhanger!"

We can't wait! •

CHARGED WITH THE UNENVIABLE JOB OF ADDING SOME
COLOR TO *THE WALKING DEAD'S* CHEEKS, COLORIST
DAVE STEWART KEEPS BRINGING A NEW LEASE OF LIFE
TO THE ICONIC COMIC BOOK'S EYE-POPPING COVERS.
WORDS & INTERVIEW: RICH MATTHEWS

If you ever watched superhero drama *Heroes* – another great continuing drama, at least for a couple of seasons – you'll have seen Dave Stewart's work on the small screen. The multi-Eisner Award-winning colorist was the man who gave Tim Sale's onscreen paintings their striking colors. Of course, as fans of *The Walking Dead* since before it reanimated itself onto television, we're already more than familiar with Stewart's incredible talent in an area of comic art that is often overlooked, especially when you consider how important it is to bringing marquee names such as Spider-Man, Superman and the Hulk to vivid, splash-page life. Yes, we know that *The Walking Dead* is drawn by Charlie Adlard in black and white, but before you open up any issue of necrotic melodrama, the first thing you see is the brilliant cover art – in striking, often chilling, color. The man responsible for that since issue 115 is Stewart.

"A cover image has to have a enough of a hook to grab someone's eye on the shelf," says Stewart. "That can be in the strength of the illustration, concept, or the vibrancy of the colors. You can stand in the comic shop and look at all the covers, and spot the images that really stand out. I think once the hook is set, the skill of the artist should finish reeling them in. Interest is created at different levels of viewing and good coloring can seal the deal."

Been There, Done That

Stewart has colored just about every book you can think of in his time working for Marvel, DC, Dark Horse and Image – you name it, he's done it. As well as all the big guns, his most memorable work has been for Mike Mignola on the *Hellboy* titles.

"I was into comics when I was a kid – the *X-Men*, *Spider-Man*, *Captain America*, *Hulk*, *Ambush Bug*..." Stewart smiles. "I was an artistic kid and started making my own comics when I was 11 or 12 years old. And I just kept drawing. Ironically, I always wondered how comics were colored – I thought it was by airbrush or something like that. Little did I know I'd find out – and then some!"

"A cover image has to have a enough of a hook to grab someone's eye on the shelf... Good coloring can seal the deal."

◇◇◇◇◇

Stewart got his formative experience of comic book production while he was still a student.

"I got into coloring when my college Photoshop teacher at Portland Community College, Mark Conahan, and I figured out how to color comic pages on our own," he explains. "Before I knew it, I was scanning in black and white art by other artists and coloring it at home on my Mac."

They may have been homemade, but those colored pages were impressive enough for another of Stewart's design teachers to grab the bull by the horns and set Stewart on the path towards a career in the industry.

"My teacher, Sharon Bronzan, had some contacts at Dark Horse Comics and set up a design internship for me in the summer," Stewart nods.

DAVE STEWART
FACT FILE

NAME: Dave Stewart
PROFESSION: Colorist
PLACE OF BIRTH: USA
BIOGRAPHY: Something of a legend in the comic book coloring business, Dave Stewart has won Best Colorist at the Eisner Comic Industry Awards no less than six times, in 2003, 2005, 2009, 2010, 2011 and 2013. He is perhaps best known for his collaboration with writer Mike Mignola on his *Hellboy* titles, but has worked on numerous other high-profile comics, including *Human Target, Conan, Captain America, Superman, Batman*, and the list goes on. He was also the man responsible for coloring Tim Sale's art in the TV series *Heroes*. He started coloring the covers of *The Walking Dead* with issue 115 in October 2013, including the special colored cover of issue one released for the 10th anniversary of the series.
FOLLOW DAVE STEWART ON TWITTER: @Dragonmnky

> "**A good coloring job acts very much like a good movie soundtrack, not drawing attention to itself, but helping to create atmosphere.**"

with the story, to emphasize the drama. You can accentuate any moment by a change in color, to emphasize a spike in mood or action."

And every book, cover and page needs to be treated with the same level of care, especially when working on art produced by lots of different artists.

"Different art styles call for different rendering techniques, so choosing the right one is very important," says Stewart. "The colors should never overpower the art. Many times, the best coloring jobs are the ones you don't notice at first. Sometimes you see an artist that is amazing [without even knowing it]."

"That turned into a job as a color separator. So, I really saw coloring as just a way into something I loved. I had a general artistic interest in color and painting, but had never really thought about separate coloring as a career. During my time working in the color separating department, I grew to appreciate the craft of comic book coloring – and before I knew it, I couldn't get enough."

The Good, The Bad, The Ugly

Like any good inker – famously labeled "tracers" in Kevin Smith's 1997 comic book world-set rom-com *Chasing Amy* – coloring is something of a hidden treasure, the irony being that bad coloring can quickly ruin the chances of a comic being successful.

"Good coloring supports the art and adds to the story," Stewart explains. "A good coloring job can act very much like a good movie soundtrack, not jumping out at you, not drawing attention to itself, but helping to set a mood, creating atmosphere. You also create a rhythm to the visuals to go

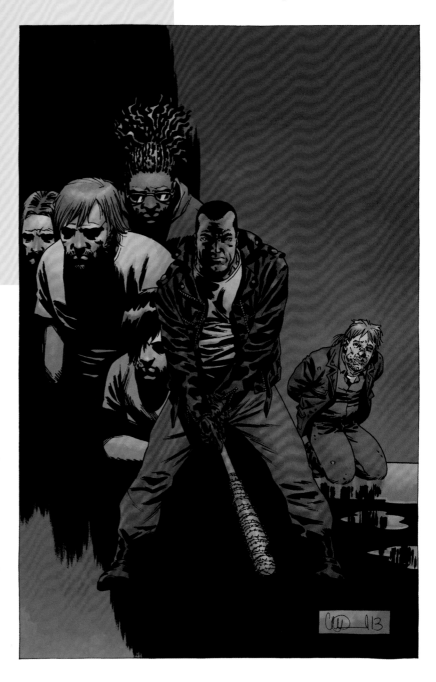

That technique is even different depending on whether you're working on covers (as on *The Walking Dead*) or on interior story pages.

"The differences between a cover versus interior pages are in the story," Stewart says. "It's static versus sequential storytelling. On the cover, you have a single graphic image to make an impact to sell the book. With interiors, you have to consider the flow of the story by emphasizing different moments."

When asked what he brings to *The Walking Dead*, Stewart's natural dry humor springs immediately to the fore.

"Color!" he laughs, before getting more serious. "I hope I bring some sense of mood, with color choices that help support what Charlie has already drawn. Its covers are the one splash of color you get in the entire book, so hopefully it adds to the reader's imagination."

Does he have a good working relationship with Adlard, then? "It's hard – he's constantly preparing for the coming plague," Stewart deadpans. "No, he's really fantastic. He has a really great style, with genius use of blacks in his work. He really captures that world. To be honest, it feels really natural to color his art. It's pretty easy."

All Work And No Play…

It turns out that Stewart and *Walking Dead* creator Robert Kirkman have collaborated on and off in the past, and *The Walking Dead* provided a perfect way for the busy pair to finally work together again.

"Robert and I work well together, but I usually have so many work commitments that it just doesn't happen very often," says Stewart. "So, when he offered me the job of coloring *The Walking Dead* covers it seemed like the perfect opportunity to do something on a regular basis. I think it's worked out really well."

That heavy workload – a rare and cherished thing in the world of comics – means that beyond his work on the covers, Stewart hasn't been able to do as much reading as he'd like, something he wryly reveals when asked what he likes most about the book.

"Well, to be honest, I haven't been able to keep up," he mock-winces. "It's been a goal of mine to get there… but I have always really liked Rick." He pauses. "Please don't tell me they killed him!"

It's clear that working on *The Walking Dead* is a fun experience for Stewart, whose natural mischievousness plays in to the work – by the time we ask him how long he sees himself working on the covers for the book, he's clearly got a case of the giggles: "Until the zombies come – I thought that was obvious. Maybe right up to the point everyone reads this interview… Yup, definitely going to get fired after this."

If that's true, he'll certainly have enough work in his portfolio to fall back on. Does he have any highlights from his career working on such a huge range of big name comics?

"*The Walking Dead* is definitely a highlight," he nods. "Then *Hellboy* and the Mignola books always come to mind when this kind of question comes up. Working with good friends and learning together is the best way to make a comic. I've worked with

> **"Charlie Adlard has a really great style, with genius use of blacks in his work. He really captures that world. It feels really natural to color his art."**

such amazing guys across my career – Fabio Moon, Gabriel Bá, JH Williams III, Darwyn Cooke, Matt Wagner, Tim Sale… I could go on."

Change For The Better

The comic book industry has undergone a lot of changes in recent years, especially with the rise of digital comics bringing them directly to the reader at the touch of a button. However, Stewart is more focused on the way the work comes into being rather than its technicalities.

> "**Learning how to color with an artist might take some serious work, but it can be rewarded with some great results.**"

"It seems like there are a lot more creator-owned projects now," he says. "I really like that because it seems like it's grown the industry in an important way. This kind of support for creator-owned work could be a new foundation for the whole business of comic books. The really interesting work definitely appears to be coming from that realm, where the creators have total freedom. *The Walking Dead* is a perfect example of passion and innovation followed by success."

So, does he have any advice for any wannabe artists and colorists out there looking at branching out into this strange new comic book world? As ever, Stewart strikes an optimistic note.

"*When* you get successful, manage your workload," he says. "I ended up working too much. At the start, you really have to take all you can, but be careful about overloading yourself. And try to recognize the good working relationships when they happen, because it's not always about business. As a colorist, look for artists to pair with. Artists, look for a colorist that gets your work and build that relationship. Learning how to color with an artist might take some serious work, but it can be rewarded with some great results."

And to see what he means, just head to your nearest comic book store or click through to your app and check out the latest issue of *The Walking Dead*. He knows what he's talking about. •

BY THE LETTER

Letterer Rus Wooton is as much an integral cog in *The Walking Dead* comic's ongoing success as Robert Kirkman and Charlie Adlard. You may not notice his influence as much, but as Wooton notes, that's kind of the point: the work of a letterer is to complement not obstruct the art, while at the same time telling the story in a coherent way. *TWDM* finds out exactly what his job entails…

INTERVIEW: Tara Bennett

A s the long-time letterer on *The Walking Dead* and *Invincible*, Rus Wooton is as synonymous a name on those titles as Robert Kirkman and Charlie Adlard. However, unless you are in the business, it might not be immediately obvious exactly what the importance of a letterer is to any title. There's sometimes a vague concept of word balloons and font placement, but lettering is an integral art form that marries the words and sequential art together into cohesive frames. Wooton is a veteran of the comic book industry, and over the years he has earned a stellar reputation in the business as a top-notch letterer.

Your dad was a career artist. Did he encourage you to follow in his footsteps?
My dad was in advertising [he designed the CNN logo – ed], so he was always drawing or creating something. And my mom was always doing some sort of crafts or decorating the house. They never discouraged me, which is good because I know people who had parents who did do that.

My dad would sometimes take me to work and I remember showing him drawings when I was a kid and he gave me critiques. I look back now and it was good, but at the same time as a kid you just wanted him to say, "Hey, that's cool!" But by the time I got into art school in college, tough critiques were nothing. (*Laughs*)

What artists inspired you?
I started with comic books. I got my first *Spider-Man* comic from my cousin when I was four. I had me a subscription to Marvel in the late 70s and remember I was into John Romita's *Spider-Man*. Dad always had illustration magazines so I was always looking at those, too. I remember the illustrator Brad Holland. Dad really liked him. In eighth grade, I had a really good art teacher who introduced me to more classical artists like Leonardo da Vinci.

There are a fair amount of self-taught artists in the comic book industry. Were you tempted by that path or did you always want to go to art school?
I knew that I wanted to go to art school to get into commercial art or illustration. When I was

in high school, I decided to get a degree in art education so I had a fallback plan if I didn't make it as an artist or freelancer. When I was in the University of South Florida, I realized I could get a double major with more fine arts classes. I did that and it got me more immersed in the art school side. I did focus on drawing.

For any budding artists out there trying to decide which path to take in regards to schooling, what's your advice to them?
I think that art school is great. If I did it again, I would push towards art and design. I enjoyed the teaching aspect, but I think if you want to go into commercial illustration, going to an art school that focuses on the commercial aspects is a good way to go.

Even if you are self-taught, I think you can get more with a fine arts degree. There are some great artists in comics who never went to art school, but I think in general a formal education is a great way to go. You open yourself up to stuff you may not even know. If you only focus on comics, I think you're going to miss out.

There are some artists who went to The Kubert School [for Cartooning and Graphic Art] in New York, and I've seen more and more professionals working now that went there. I think if someone really wants to get into comics, they should consider that place as well.

You worked for Wizard Entertainment in the late 90s. Was that your door into the comics industry?
Yeah, a big part. I took the job at Wizard to make more contacts in the business. I did freelance work for Wizard's website redesign and when they needed a second guy for the web department, they talked to me and a couple of other guys.

I didn't want to move to New York or leave the warm weather in Florida, but I figured it would be a good opportunity to immerse myself more in the comic book business. That's where I met Chris Eliopoulos, who I started working for and he taught me

how to letter. I never planned to be a letterer, but at the time it worked out well.

What do you think Chris saw in you that led him to mentor you in lettering?
I think Chris asked me to be his assistant because he knew my design sense and my work ethic. My background in design and fine arts worked together. Fine arts helps with the graphic design, and then the graphic design in turn helps the lettering.

The lettering I do, and most lettering, is digital now, so it's more of a graphic design job. Lettering with pen and ink was a calligraphy job. It used to be more artistic, and the guys who still do it with pen and ink are more like artists. I'm more of a designer. It was easy for me to pick up the mechanical part of it.

For someone that thinks lettering is just about plopping words into circles, explain the nuances of what you do.
The most important thing is that you're helping to tell the story and it's the first thing you think about. You have to make sure the reader is following the story and not getting lost in the word balloons. Most people read comic strips in the newspaper, but that's a much simpler layout than a comic book.

The key is to keep the story and not obstruct the artwork. You don't want the lettering to overpower it. You want it to complement and flow. And if I'm working on a color book, I want to complement the colorist's work and I don't want my sound effects to clash with their work. I've seen some nice sound effects, but all you *see* are the sound effects aside from the artwork itself. So it's a process of complementing the artist, then the colorist, while helping the story along.

How did you get the lettering job on *The Walking Dead*?
Robert [Kirkman] was looking for someone to take over the lettering for *The Walking Dead* and *Invincible* because he wanted

"FINE ARTS HELPS WITH THE GRAPHIC DESIGN, AND THEN THE GRAPHIC DESIGN IN TURN HELPS THE LETTERING."

to get the titles out faster. Robert was doing a good job already, and had all the established styles for both of his books, and he wanted someone to make the transition. It was a good opportunity for me because it was the first freelance lettering work I did outside of my Marvel work. It opened doors for me down the line.

Did you go in changing the lettering?
No, Robert basically wanted me to ape his style and keep a consistent look so the readers weren't jarred. I took what he had already done and tried to make it a little bit my own, but keep it consistent. I started with Issue 20, right after Michonne's appearance.

You've been on *The Walking Dead* since then, so how have you changed the lettering?
I have tried to be a little more flexible with some of the ways people are speaking to try to emphasize things more. When I first started, I was more conservative. Now I push it a little bit, keeping within a style, but pushing to make the lettering more dynamic, especially on the more impactful pages from Charlie [Adlard].

With the sound effects, I've made them more dynamic. I've laid them out differently. We just finished up issue 107 [as *TWDM* was going to press], so when there's something like shouting, I've been playing a little more with that lately to change it up and keep it fresh.

Explain the collaborative process working with Adlard and Kirkman on an issue.
I get pages from Charlie and go to town. One of the great aspects of working with Charlie on *The Walking Dead* is his storytelling is so solid that I can letter without worrying much about covering up art or fretting over balloon placement. He's adept at laying out the pages and panels and allowing room for Robert's dialogue. Otherwise, if there's anything specific, it may come from Robert in the script. As I'm going through the script, he may have notes to try this here or there.

"NOT OBSTRUCTING THE ARTWORK IS KEY. YOU DON'T WANT THE LETTERING TO OVERPOWER IT. YOU WANT IT TO COMPLEMENT AND FLOW."

OPPOSITE PAGE, TOP: *The Walking Dead* is a dialogue heavy comic, but Wooton always finds the right way of working it into the artwork. THIS PAGE, TOP & RIGHT: Wooton's use of sound effects has changed over the past 90 issues or so he's been involved with the comic. ABOVE: Abraham's long speech is clean and easy to read; in other words, it's perfectly represented on the page.

What's your average turnaround to letter an issue?

The letterer usually gets the pages last. Best case, I always prefer to have a week. It doesn't take a week for me to letter it, but because I'm working on multiple books a month, I like to have a week to juggle things around. Usually it's only a few days. Worst case is when it's needed the next day.

How many titles do you letter on average?

Off the top of my head, I'm lettering eight to 10 titles a month. It can go more than that or less depending on schedules.

Where do you see lettering going in the digital age of comics?

There's been a shift with people doing a monthly book all digitally. It's something I've thought about, and maybe I'll work it into my own projects; seeing what it would be like to letter in a more traditional manner with pen and ink, but doing it on the computer. Instead of using fonts, it would be lettering by hand, but doing it digitally so you can make changes and corrections crisper and cleaner. I wouldn't be surprised if we see more of that and more of that artistic flair that lettering used to have.

Tell us about some of the other titles you letter.

A recent book I really liked is *Butcher Baker, The Righteous Maker*. It's Joe Casey and Mike Huddleston's book that just came out in trade paperback a couple months ago. Joe's books end up being

"I PUSH THE LETTERING A LITTLE BIT NOW, SO IT'S MORE DYNAMIC, ESPECIALLY ON THE MORE IMPACTFUL PAGES FROM CHARLIE ADLARD."

TOP: Wooton hard at work. ABOVE & ABOVE LEFT: These panels, from issues 105 and 106, are two of Wooton's recent favorites. LEFT & BELOW: Here are perfect examples of Wooton's work: great placement and variety in style of the lettering, illustrating everything from general dialogue to shouting, exclamations and sound effects.

some of the toughest books to letter for me, but also the ones I enjoy the most even though it's more work and more labor intensive. I'm also proud of *Fear Agent* and *The Last Days Of American Crime*.

Do you have any advice that you could give to the next generation of artists trying to break into the business?

A lot of artists, writers and letterers want to break into comics instead of just doing comics. If you do comics, you'll have something to show people. It's not about saying, "Give me a job," but more learning *on* the job. Do something, get better at it and hopefully people will notice. There is all this access to put stuff out there and get it out in front of people with self-publishing – Kickstarter, DeviantArt or even webcomics. Just do it and network. •

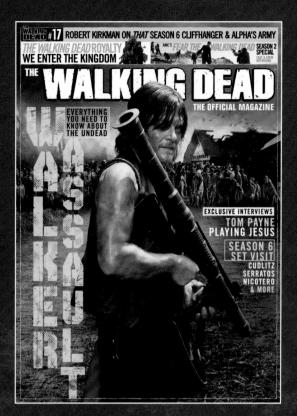

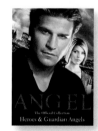
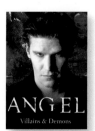